knitting smitten

knitting
smitten

20 FRESH AND FUNKY HAND-KNIT DESIGNS

Jessica Biscoe

Quadrille
PUBLISHING

Photography by Keiko Oikawa

contents

WHAT'S INSIDE...

introduction

As a young child I always had a desire to create. From sketching my pet hamster at age three, to raiding my mum's art cupboard in the summer holidays, I was forever making things… or so I thought. My efforts earned me the nickname 'Messy Jessy', so the success of my artistic endeavors is debatable!

Fast forward to 2008, business degree in hand, I was thrown head-first into the corporate world and soon found myself yearning to create again. The resurgence of the craft movement at this time was a key inspiration, and I felt compelled to equip myself with a traditional skill that would allow me to create something tangible, and useful, with my own hands.

Knitting caught my imagination (thanks to an inspired birthday present) and it's safe to say I quickly became obsessed, devouring every book, blog, tutorial and article I could find. From the outset I was particularly interested in the design process and different construction techniques; I needed to know how and why, preferring to create my own pieces, rather than follow patterns.

Putting this book together has been a hugely enjoyable experience that has immersed me in those design elements that I love the most. I particularly enjoyed deciding on the best stitch patterns and shaping methods for the Ballerina Slippers and Hedgehog Paperweight. I also took pleasure in creating the larger homeware items, such as the Triangle Motif Throw, which has a lovely drape and luxurious texture — perfect for an evening on the sofa with a good book!

I really hope you enjoy making and using these projects as much as I did creating them.

Happy knitting!

Jessica

x

Knitting Basics

• Knitting kit • Choosing yarns • Deciphering knitting patterns • Working from knitting charts • Making a slipknot • Casting on • Working the knit stitch • Working the purl stitch • Casting off • Decreasing • Increasing • Measuring tension • Tips for novice knitters

Knitting Kit

The most basic knitting kit can consist of nothing more than two needles and a tape measure, but there is a selection of other useful items that are good for a knitter to have in their arsenal.

Knitting needles

Knitting needles come in a variety of lengths and thicknesses, depending on the yarn you are knitting with and how many stitches you want to hold on your needle. The general rule of thumb is that when you knit with really thick yarn you will need to use thicker needles, and when you knit with finer yarn you are likely to use thinner needles. When you buy yarn, the label around the ball, hank or skein always has a suggested needle size on it recommended by the manufacturer, but you can always play around with this if you want a tighter or looser stitch than the one suggested. You can also get circular needles for knitting in the round. Basically, these are two shorter needles connected by a long nylon wire. You can use circular needles for knitting in rows as well as working in the round, just make sure at the end of each row you swap the needles over in your hands and knit back the way you've just come, rather than continue to knit round and round.

Stitch holders

A few stitch holders are very useful for when knitting garments. Whenever you have stitches that at any point are not being worked – around a neckline on a sweater, for example – then slip these unworked stitches onto a stitch holder in order to hold them securely while you continue with a different section of knitting. These stitches may then be returned later to the needles from the stitch holder once you are ready to work with them again. Safety pins are a good, inexpensive alternative to stitch holders for holding just a small number of stitches.

Cable needles

Cable needles are short open-ended needles – sometimes with a shallow v-shape in the centre – that hold a few stitches at a time, mainly used when you make the forward or back twist in a decorative cable.

Needle gauge

If you have a collection of vintage knitting needles, which can be picked up from charity shops or car boot sales, a gauge is really useful. As the old imperial sizing system isn't the same as new metric one, this is the best way to confirm the size of any needle.

Row counter

A tiny cylinder with rotating numbers that slips on to one knitting needle. Each time you complete a row or round, change the number so you know where you are in your pattern at all times.

Stitch markers

You don't have to buy purpose-made stitch markers for your kit, but I adore my tiny teacup stitch markers. You can use pretty much anything to hand – coloured elastic bands, loops of contrast yarn or even paperclips – as stitch markers to denote the beginning of rounds when knitting on circular needles, key places in a repeat stitch pattern or the point of an increase or decrease when shaping.

Yarn needle

Always keep a few blunt-ended yarn needles – darning or tapestry needles – with an eye that is large enough to thread yarn through for seaming and stitching up knitted garments. It's preferable not to use needles that are too fine as often you find yourself stitching through the knitted yarn and splitting it. A bodkin, which is similar to a needle but is very thick with a big eye, is perfect for stitching up chunkier knitted garments.

Pins and safety pins

These are always useful for pinning seams together before you stitch them, so you know you're sewing evenly.

Tape measure

A dressmaker's tape measure is crucial for checking your knitted tension. You may also find some designer's patterns give centimetre or inch measurements instead of counting the number of rows.

choosing yarns

There is an amazing array of hand-knit yarns available to the home knitter, in a kaleidoscope of colours and a range of different thicknesses. If you don't fancy using the specific recommended yarn for a particular pattern, another yarn of the same thickness may be substituted. So, if I recommend using an aran weight yarn you can substitute this for another aran yarn. Just make sure you work a tension swatch and match the recommended tension given at the beginning of the pattern.

superfine or lace weight yarn

average knitted tension over 10cm: 27–32 stitches

recommended needle size: 2.25–3.25mm

4ply weight yarn

average knitted tension over 10cm: 23–26 stitches

recommended needle size: 3.25–3.75mm

double-knitting weight yarn

average knitted tension over 10cm: 21–24 stitches

recommended needle size: 3.75–4.5mm

You will find a handy conversion chart on the inside front flap of this book, listing all the standard knitting needle sizes in metric, UK imperial and US.

aran weight yarn

average knitted tension over 10cm: 16–20 stitches

recommended needle size: 4.5–5.5mm

chunky weight yarn

average knitted tension over 10cm: 12–15 stitches

recommended needle size: 5.5–8mm

superchunky weight yarn

average knitted tension over 10cm: 6–11 stitches

recommended needle size: 8mm and larger

Whatever yarn you choose, the label or ball band will provide information on recommended needle sizes, tension and the weight and length of the yarn in metres or yards. When buying more than one ball of any yarn, check they all have the same dye lot number. Although the balls may all look the same, there can be subtle colour differences between batches, which may show when knitted. While knitting a project, keep a note of the dye lot number in case you need to buy more yarn.

Deciphering Knitting Patterns

To the uninitiated, a knitting pattern can look like a string of incomprehensible goobledygook. Each line of a knitting pattern is like a recipe and once you understand the format and have learnt the terminology, knitting patterns are a breeze to follow.

A pattern works through all elements of the project, giving the necessary instructions for every part. Beginning with the size of needles, weight of yarn and number of stitches to cast on, the pattern then continues to outline, row by row, the stitch pattern to follow and indicates when any shaping or other details, such as buttonholes, must be worked. It takes a while to become familiar with the language of knitting patterns, so on this page and on the inside back flap of this book is a handy list of the most commonly used abbreviations.

When following any pattern, be aware of the different usage of round brackets ( ) and square brackets [ ]. Round brackets indicate the different measurements or stitches given for multiple sizes. The first size is always shown outside the round brackets and the remaining sizes within them. Square brackets in knitting patterns have nothing to do with sizing but relate to repeating instructions.

ABBREVIATIONS

alt	alternate
beg	begin(ning)
cont	continue(ing)
cm	centimetre(s)
dec	decrease(s)(ing)
foll	follow(s)(ing)
g	gram(s)
g st	garter stitch
in	inch(es)
inc	increase(s)(ing)
k or K	knit
k2tog	knit next 2 stitches together
kfb	knit into front and back of next stitch
LH	left-hand
m	metre(s)
m1	make one (see page 34)
mm	millimetre(s)
p or P	purl
p2tog	purl next 2 stitches together
patt(s)	pattern(s)
psso	pass slipped stitch over
p2sso	pass 2 slipped stitches over
rem	remain(s)(ing)
rep	repeat(s)(ing)
rev st st	reverse stocking stitch
RH	right-hand
RS	right side
skpo	slip 1, knit 1, pass slipped stitch over
sl	slip
sm	slip marker
ssk	slip next 2 sts knitwise, one at a time, insert left needle into front of these 2 sts and knit them together
st(s)	stitch(es)
st st	stocking stitch
tbl	through back loop(s)
tog	together
WS	wrong side
yf or yfwd	yarn forward (as if to purl)
yon	yarn over needle
yrn	yarn round needle
[ ]	work instructions within square brackets as many times as directed

working from knitting charts

Instead of being written out row by row using standard knitting terminology, a colour motif or repeat pattern can also be represented as a chart on graph paper. All the colourwork motifs for the projects in this book are given as charts – so at a glance, you can see exactly what the finished result should look like.

Colourwork instructions can either be written out in full within the pattern or represented as a chart. The various shades of yarn that make up the colourwork motif or repeat pattern are represented either as a symbol or – more commonly – as a shaded colour, specified in a key.

Each square of the chart represents one stitch, and each line of squares represents one row of knitting. With both types of chart the right-side rows (or odd-numbered rows) are read from right to left, while the wrong-side rows (or even-numbered rows) are read from left to right. The rows of the chart are read from the bottom to the top.

For both the Cosy Mittens adorned with cute squirrels on pages 54–59 and the fabulous Flamingo Cushion on pages 100–105, the colourwork motifs were applied onto the finished knitted piece using duplicate stitch (also known as Swiss darning). You

will find instructions on how to work duplicate stitch on page 104.

For the Triangle Motif Throw on pages 106–109 and the Chevron Cushion on pages 114–117, the colour chart shows the 8-stitch pattern repeat that is knitted as many times as instructed, rather than applied to the finished work.

KEY FOR CHART

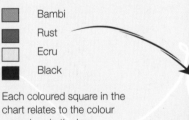

Bambi
Rust
Ecru
Black

Each coloured square in the chart relates to the colour yarn given in the key

Each square of the chart represents one stitch

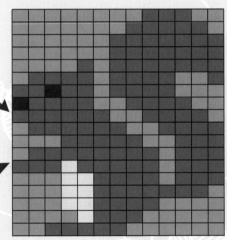

Each line of squares represents one row of knitting

starting to knit

As for many crafts, within knitting there are various different methods you can employ in order to achieve the same end result. Knitting is practised all around the world and varying techniques have evolved in different regions. There is no right way or wrong way to knit. The best way is the method that you find most comfortable, so when you are first learning to knit try out different hand positions until you hit upon the one that comes most naturally to you.

With the exception of making a slipknot, two methods are demonstrated for each of the basic techniques shown in this section. The first is the method most commonly used in England and the US, where the working yarn is manipulated with the right hand and which is shown on the left in orange yarn. The second is the one more regularly employed in Continental Europe, where the yarn is moved by the left hand and which is pictured on the right in grey yarn.

making a slipknot

The slip knot is the very first stitch you make when starting any piece of knitting. Without the slip knot you won't be able to work a single row as it acts as the anchor for all knitting, so this is the first technique you need to practise and master. Once you know how, making a slip knot is simple.

1 Make the yarn into a loose figure-of-eight shape, holding the tail end of the yarn in your right hand and the loop of yarn in your left hand.

2 Pass the working yarn from your right hand through the loop in your left hand, ensuring that you keep hold of the tail end of the yarn with your right hand and hold the new loop of yarn with your left hand.

3 Pull this new loop of yarn through the left-hand loop, keeping hold of both the yarn ends in your right hand. This forms a slip knot. Place the slip knot onto your knitting needle and pull the ends to tighten. This counts as your first stitch.

casting on

Casting on is the term used for when you make the first row of stitches on your knitting needle. No matter what you are making, the pattern will always start with the instruction to cast on a certain number of stitches. There are countless different ways of casting on, but two of the most common methods – and the ones I use most often – are the knit-on and long-tail cast-on.

1 With the slip knot on the left needle – counts as the first stitch – insert the right needle tip up into the stitch, crossing the left needle over the right needle.

2 With your right hand wrap the working end of the yarn – the end attached to the ball – round the back of the right needle in an anti-clockwise motion.

3 Catching the working yarn that has just been wound round the needle, bring the right needle tip underneath the loop on the left needle and to the front of the stitch.

4 Pull the new loop further through. Insert the left needle tip up into the loop on the right needle. Slide the right needle out and pull the working end of the yarn to tighten. This counts as the second stitch.

5 To make subsequent stitches, insert the right needle tip between the last two stitches on the left needle and not into the stitch. Wrap and pull the yarn through and place on the left needle as before.

The long-tail cast on method is a useful technique to know. The most popular method of casting on used in continental Europe, this technique gives a firm cast-on edge. It is called the long-tail cast on as you need to leave a tail end of yarn long enough to make all the required stitches. Placing the slipknot on two needles prevents the cast-on edge becoming too tight.

1 Place the slipknot on two needles. Wrap the tail end yarn over your left thumb. Hold the working yarn over your index finger and use your middle fingers to add tension.

2 Take the needles down and under the loop around your thumb, swooping upwards towards the strand over your index finger.

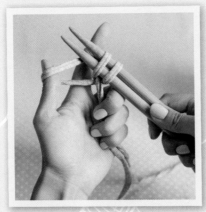

3 Next take the needle up and over the loop around your index finger, swooping downwards this time.

4 Draw the yarn wrapped over your index finger caught on the needles through the loop around your thumb to form a stitch.

5 Slip the new loop off your thumb and tighten the newly cast-on stitch on the needles. Repeat these steps until you have the required number of stitches.

Working the Knit Stitch

This is the key basic stitch to learn. Most other knitting stitches are a variation on the knit stitch, so this simple four-step process is an important technique to master. The most common technique for working the knit stitch is known as the English method, which is shown on this page. Opposite is an alternative technique called the Continental method. With the English method, your right hand controls the flow and tension of the working yarn, wrapping it around the needle.

1 Holding the needle full of stitches in your left hand, insert the right needle tip up through the first stitch on the left needle so the right needle crosses behind the left.

2 With your right hand, wrap the working yarn in an anti-clockwise motion round the back of the right needle and then between the tips of both crossed needles.

3 With the right needle tip, catch the working yarn that has just been wound round and bring it underneath the loop on the left needle. Pull the working yarn through to the front of the stitch.

4 Slide the existing stitch off the left needle, leaving the newly formed stitch on the right needle. Repeat these steps until all the stitches on the left needle have been worked.

The Continental method for working the knit stitch uses a different knitting position from the English method. With this technique you hold the yarn static in your left hand and move the right needle to catch and pull the strand of yarn through the loops on the left needle to form the new stitch. For a lot of knitters, they find this Continental method a quicker way to knit.

1 Holding the needle full of stitches in your left hand, insert the right needle tip up through the first stitch on the left needle so the right needle crosses behind the left.

2 Keeping a firm tension, catch the working yarn with the right needle tip by swooping under the strand.

3 With the right needle tip, pull the working yarn through the existing stitch. If necessary, hold the strand in place on the needle with your right finger.

4 Slide the existing stitch off the left needle, leaving the newly formed stitch on the right needle. Repeat these steps until all the stitches on the left needle have been worked.

working the purl stitch

The next technique to learn is the purl stitch, which looks exactly like the reverse of a knit stitch. As perfect partners, the knit and purl stitches are used in combination to create endless stitch patterns. Again, the most common technique for working the purl stitch is the English method. When knitting the purl stitch the working yarn is held at the front of the work rather than to the back, as with the knit stitch. Also, whereas the right needle is inserted into a stitch from front to back when working the knit stitch, with the purl stitch you insert the needle from back to front.

1 With the working yarn at the front, insert the right needle tip up through the first stitch on the left needle so the right needle crosses in front of the left needle.

2 With your right hand, wrap the working yarn in an anti-clockwise motion round the back of the right needle and then between the tips of both crossed needles.

3 With the right needle tip, catch the working yarn that has just been wound round and bring it underneath the loop on the left needle. Pull the working yarn through to the back of the stitch.

4 Slide the existing stitch off the left needle, leaving the newly formed stitch on the right needle. Repeat these steps until all the stitches on the left needle have been worked.

1 Holding the needle full of stitches in your left hand, insert the right needle tip up through the first stitch on the left needle so the right needle crosses in front of the left.

2 Keeping a firm tension, catch the working yarn with the right needle tip by swooping under the strand.

3 With the right needle tip, pull the working yarn through the existing stitch. If necessary, hold the strand in place on the needle with your right finger.

4 Slide the existing stitch off the left needle, leaving the newly formed stitch on the right needle. Repeat these steps until all the stitches on the left needle have been worked.

casting off

When a piece of knitting is finished you need to take it off the needles. So the work does not unravel, the stitches must be cast off. Whether your knitting tension is tight or loose, keep your stitches looser than usual when casting off. This will stop the work from puckering at the cast-off edge and spoiling your knitting. To keep your cast-off loose, try using a slightly larger size knitting needle to cast off with.

1 When casting off knitwise, knit two stitches in the usual way. Insert the left needle tip into the front of the first of these two knitted stitches.

2 Carefully lift the first knitted stitch over the second and over the tip of the right needle.

3 Release the stitch from the left needle tip to leave one stitch on the right needle. Knit one more stitch then repeat the lifting of the first stitch on the right needle over the second stitch and off the needle.

4 When you have been casting off for a full row and have one stitch left on the right needle, cut the working yarn, leaving a fair length so your knitting doesn't unravel.

5 Loosen the final stitch to make a bigger loop and remove the knitting needle. Pass the cut end of the working yarn through this last loop and tighten.

1 When casting off knitwise, knit two stitches in the usual way. Insert the left needle tip into the front of the first of these two knitted stitches.

2 Carefully lift the first knitted stitch over the second and over the tip of the right needle.

3 Release the stitch from the left needle tip to leave one stitch on the right needle. Knit one more stitch then repeat the lifting of the first stitch on the right needle over the second stitch and off the needle.

4 When you have been casting off for a full row and have one stitch left on the right needle, cut the working yarn, leaving a fair length so your knitting doesn't unravel.

5 Loosen the final stitch to make a bigger loop and remove the knitting needle. Pass the cut end of the working yarn through this last loop and tighten.

Decreasing – Knit 2 together

The easiest way to decrease the number of stitches in a row, is to knit the two stitches together in one new stitch. This is as simple as it sounds. The abbreviation for this is 'k2tog' which just means 'knit 2 together'. As with most things in knitting there are several ways to decrease stitches; this is the most straightforward – and most common – method.

1 When placing the right needle tip into the stitches on the left needle, instead of picking up just one stitch, pick up the next two stitches at the same time.

2 Wrap the yarn round the right needle as you would with a normal knit stitch in an anti-clockwise motion from back to front.

3 Catching the yarn that you've just wound round, bring the right needle tip through both the loops on the left needle.

4 Slide the two stitches off the left needle to make one new stitch on the right needle.

1 When placing the right needle tip into the stitches on the left needle, instead of picking up just one stitch, pick up the next two stitches at the same time.

2 Wrap the yarn round the right needle as you would with a normal knit stitch in an anti-clockwise motion.

3 Catching the yarn that you've just wound round, bring the right needle tip through both the loops on the left needle.

4 Slide the two stitches off the left needle to make one new stitch on the right needle.

Decreasing – Knit 2 together through back loop

This is another really simple way to decrease the number of stitches on your needles. It's very similar to k2tog, however instead of knitting up into the two stitches as you would do with a k2tog, you knit down into the back of the stitches. The abbreviation 'k2tog tbl' just means 'knit 2 together through back loops'.

1 Place the right needle tip through the two stitches at the back of the work. Push the needle up further through the two stitches.

2 Wrap the yarn round the needle as you would with a normal knit stitch, in an anti-clockwise motion.

3 Catching the yarn that you've just looped round, pull the tip of the needle through both of the stitches being knitted together.

4 Slide both stitches off the left needle leaving just the one new stitch on the right needle.

1 Place the right needle tip through the two stitches at the back of the work. Push the needle up further through the two stitches.

2 Wrap the yarn round the needle as you would with a normal knit stitch, in an anti-clockwise motion.

3 Catching the yarn that you've just looped round, pull the tip of the needle through both of the stitches being knitted together.

4 Slide both stitches off the left needle leaving just the one new stitch on the right needle.

incrEaSinG – knit Front & BacK

When you increase within a row of knitting you can simply cast on one stitch at the appropriate point, however this way of increasing gives a far neater finish and is often used in patterns for garments. With this increase method you knit into the front and back of the same stitch, making two stitches from one stitch.

1 Insert the needle into the stitch as usual, wrap the yarn round and pull it through, but do not slip the loop off the needle.

2 Keeping the new stitch on the right needle, knit into the same stitch on the left needle but into the back of the stitch.

3 Wrap the yarn round the right needle tip as with any knit stitch, from back to front in an anti-clockwise motion.

4 Catch the yarn that has been wrapped round and bring the right needle tip through the stitch.

5 Slide the old stitch off the left needle. You now have two new stitches on the right needle.

1 Insert the needle into the stitch as usual, wrap the yarn round and pull it through, but do not slip the loop off the needle.

2 Keeping the new stitch on the right needle, knit into the same stitch on the left needle but into the back of the stitch.

3 Wrap the yarn round the right needle tip as with any knit stitch, in an anti-clockwise motion.

4 Catch the yarn that has been wrapped round and bring the right needle tip through the stitch.

5 Slide the old stitch off the left needle. You now have two new stitches on the right needle.

increasing – make one

Within a knitting pattern, when you are instructed to make an increase with the command 'm1' this abbreviation means 'make one stitch'. The method for making this new stitch is the same whatever point within the row you are at. The result is that where you previously had just one stitch, you will now have two stitches.

1 With the left needle tip, lift the horizontal bar between the unworked and worked stitches. If the picked up loop is too tight to knit easily, loosen it with your fingers.

2 Insert the right needle tip into this new loop on the left needle through the back of the loop – this twists the loop so a hole does not form under it.

3 Wrap the working yarn in an anti-clockwise motion round the back of the right needle and then between the tips of both crossed needles, as usual.

4 With the right needle tip, catch the working yarn and bring it underneath the loop on the left needle. Pull the yarn through to the front of the stitch, as usual.

5 Slide the picked up stitch off the left needle. When you count up the stitches at the end of this increase row, you will have one more stitch than in the preceding row.

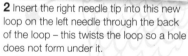

1 With the left needle tip, lift the horizontal bar between the unworked and worked stitches. If the picked up loop is too tight to knit easily, loosen it with your fingers.

2 Insert the right needle tip into this new loop on the left needle through the back of the loop – this twists the loop so a hole does not form under it.

3 Wrap the working yarn in an anti-clockwise motion round the back of the right needle, as usual.

4 With the right needle tip, catch the working yarn and bring it underneath the loop on the left needle. Pull the yarn through to the front of the stitch, as usual.

5 Slide the picked up stitch off the left needle. When you count up the stitches at the end of this increase row, you will have one more stitch than in the preceding row.

measuring tension

In the same way that everyone's handwriting is slightly different, so is everyone's knitting. Each knitter works to their own tension depending on how they hold and control the yarn – some knitters' tension can be tight, some knitters' tension can be loose while others can be just right.

Working and measuring a tension swatch before you start to knit any pattern is very important, especially if you are a beginner. The point of it is just to ensure that you are knitting in the same tension the pattern is written in so you know that your handknit will come out the right size and as the designer intended it.

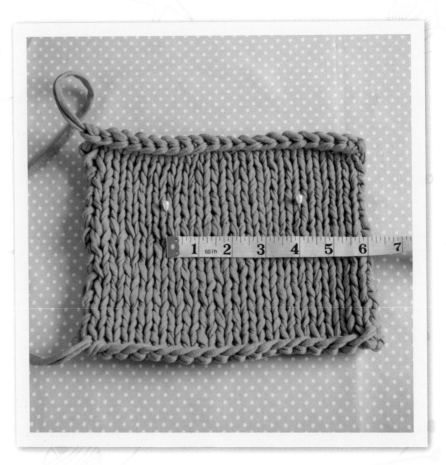

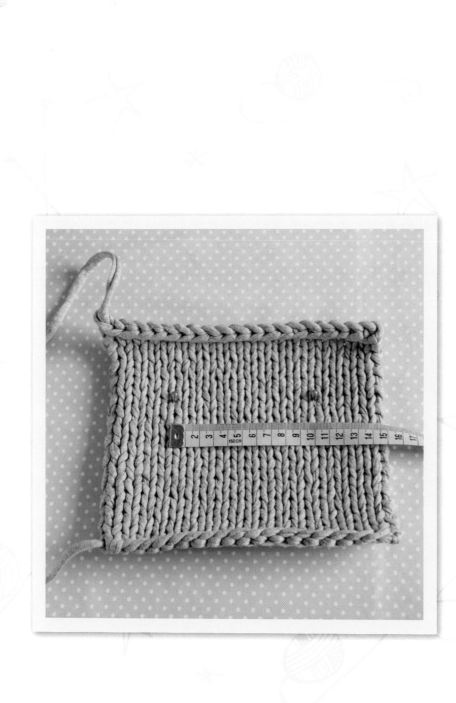

If your tension matches that given at the beginning of the pattern, then your project will knit up to the exact size required. Achieving an exact tension is especially important when knitting garments, however it is less vital for some of the projects in this book, such as the Maiden Braid Bracelets on pages 72–75 as they do not need to fit the body closely and can be adjusted.

The tension given at the beginning of a knitting pattern is almost always written giving the number of stitches and rows in a 10cm x 10cm square. It's best if you knit a few centimetres extra so you can take a measurement from the centre of the swatch.

When you have knitted up a good sized square, lay it out on a flat surface and – using a tape measure and some pins – mark out a 10cm x 10cm square. Count the number of stitches within the pins. Each stitch looks like a 'V' and you will find generally that you will count more rows (vertically) than stitches (horizontally). This is because knit stitches are usually wider than they are tall.

Once you have counted the stitches and the rows within this 10cm x 10cm square, compare your tension to that given in the pattern. If it matches, that's great, you can begin to knit the pattern. If it doesn't match, don't worry. If you find that you have more stitches within the 10cm than the pattern states this means that you are knitting a little too tightly and so should try knitting another tension swatch using slightly thicker needles. If you find that you have fewer stitches within the 10cm then this means that you are knitting a little too loosely and so should try knitting another tension swatch using slightly thinner needles. It may seem painstaking to begin with, but it's definitely worth getting right.

tips for novice knitters

Knitting is a relaxing hobby, so enjoy the craft. Don't get bogged down trying to master instantly every technique and don't panic if you go wrong or drop a stitch. Have fun playing around with the endless possibilities of knitting.

PRACTISE HOLDING THE YARN

Wrap the working end of the yarn (the one attached to the ball) once around the index finger of your right hand. Everyone has their own way of holding the yarn, but while you are learning this is the easiest way to keep the yarn in the correct place. It also helps to produce an even tension when knitting.

WORK A TENSION SWATCH

It's so important to get into the habit of knitting a tension swatch. No matter how tempting it is to dive in and begin the pattern, you need to know that you are working to the correct tension. If your tension isn't right, you may end up with an ill-fitting garment. Use the tension swatch for practising your basic stitches, as well as casting on and off. You can always put any tension squares to use afterwards by stitching lots together to make a scarf or a throw.

READ THE PATTERN

When starting any knitting project, take the time to read through all the instructions beforehand so you know will know what to expect. As you work through the pattern, either tick off where you are or keep a row counter handy so you don't get lost or forget which part you've already knitted.

FIX ANY MISTAKES

Most mistakes in knitting are easily fixed. Learning to do this will give you confidence and ease the frustration when something doesn't look quite right. Ripping out all your hard work is called frogging and should be a last resort—for your sanity more than anything else!

TUTORIAL VIDEOS

When you don't have a knitter friend nearby to help you, watching tutorial videos online can offer quick answers and explanations. You will find a helpful selection on my own website, www.jessicabiscoe.co.uk.

JOIN A KNITTING GROUP

Find a knitting buddy or join a group. When teaching yourself to knit, at times it can be frustrating so it's good to be surrounded by others who can answer questions and offer help. You can learn just by watching other knitters. It's also a good way to meet people, share ideas and feel inspired by what they are creating.

IMPROVISE

Hair grips and safety pins make fantastic stitch holders and cable needles. And, if you don't have any stitch markers yet, a knotted loop of scrap yarn will do the trick.

STRAIGHT OR ROUND

Circular needles are used to knit in the round but they can also be used in place of straight needles to knit in rows. I have a set of interchangeable circular needles, with different length cables, that I use for all my knitting. A long circular cable is useful if you don't have straight needles quite long enough for your project.

SIGN UP TO RAVELRY

There's a whole world of patterns and helpful, knowledgeable folk waiting for you at www.ravelry.com.

COUNT YOUR STITCHES

Counting your stitches at the end of each row means you'll know immediately when something has gone wrong and you can promptly correct the mistake.

SUPERSIZE ME

When you're just starting out, super-chunky needles and yarn are great to practise with. The stitches will be big and clear and your project will grow in no time at all. Cast on 20 stitches and knit back and forth to create a garter stitch scarf.

STASH BUSTING!

Think of ways to use up leftover yarn, make gifts for your friends and express your creativity.

LEARN THE ABBREVIATIONS

You'll find a list of the most common knitting abbreviations handily placed on the back flap of this book for easy reference!

EXPERIMENT

Knitting needles come in lots of different materials: plastic, bamboo, aluminium, and wood, to name a few. Experiment with each type of needle to see which you prefer. Bamboo and wooden needles are 'stickier' and will grip onto stitches – good if you are prone to the odd dropped stitch. Aluminium and plastic needles can be slippier, but will allow you to knit faster and smoother as you gain confidence. It's all a matter of preference!

knits to wear

- Slouch hat • Ballerina slippers
- Ribbed bobble hat • Cosy mittens
- Moss stitch cowl • Diamond leg warmers
- Winter cape

slouch hat

This slouch hat is the ultimate quick knit. After just a few hours of knitting, you'll be winter-ready. It's a brilliant start project if you are new to knitting on circular needles, too.

SUPPLIES

SIZE:
One size to fit all

Length, unstretched: 27cm

Circumference, unstretched: 44cm

YARN:
Debbie Bliss *Luxury Donegal Tweed Chunky*

Colour: Heather (05)

Amount: 1 x 100g ball

KNITTING NEEDLES & EXTRAS:
6.5mm circular knitting needle, 40cm long

Stitch marker

TENSION:
12 sts and 19 rows to 10cm (4in) measured over st st using 6.5mm needles.

ABBREVIATIONS:
See either page 14 or the inside back-cover flap.

TO MAKE THE SLOUCH HAT

Cast on 52 sts.

Place a marker at beg of round and join for working in the round, being careful no stitches are twisted.

(See right for tips on working in the round.)

Round 1: K52.

Continue working st st (knit every round) until work measures 26cm.

Shape crown

Round 1: *K2tog; rep from * to end of round. (26 sts)

Round 2: *K2tog; rep from * to end of round. (13 sts.)

Cut off yarn, leaving a long yarn tail. Thread the yarn tail onto a yarn needle, pass the needle through the remaining live stitches, pull to draw closed and secure.

TO FINISH

Weave in any stray yarn ends.

WORKING IN THE ROUND

Cast on the required number of stitches. If the stitches are twisted on the needles and wire (**1**) then take a moment to make sure the stitches are all sitting neatly and evenly around the needle (**2**).

Place a stitch marker on the right needle to indicate the beginning of the first round and knit the first stitch on the left needle to join the stitches into a round (**3**).

Continue working the stitches in rounds, with the right side always facing you, and remembering to slip the stitch marker from the left needle onto the right needle at the beginning of each round (**4**).

TECHNIQUES USED

Knit stitch –
see pages 22–23
K2tog decrease –
see pages 28–29
Working in the round –
see right

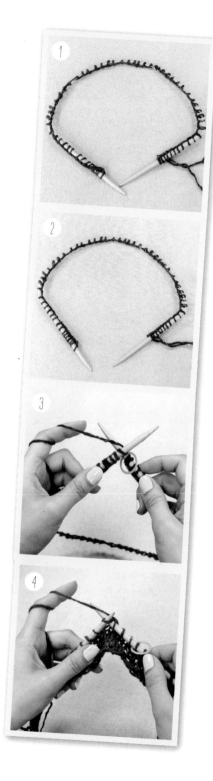

ballerina slippers

These cute, girly slippers make the perfect indoor shoes, and are deceptively simple to knit. Worked entirely on straight needles with just one seam, you can have toasty toes in no time at all.

SUPPLIES

TECHNIQUES *USED*

M1 increase – see pages 34–35
SSK decrease – see page 52
K2tog decrease – see pages 28–29
Garter stitch seam – see page 49
Mattress stitch seam – see page 49
Whip stitch – see page 96

SIZE:
To fit average women's shoe sizes

Length, unstretched: 24cm

Width, unstretched: 10cm

YARN:
Debbie Bliss *Rialto Chunky*

Main colour: Ruby (015)

Amount: 2 x 50g balls

KNITTING NEDDLES & EXTRAS:
Pair of 6mm knitting needles

Pair of 4mm knitting needles, for bows (optional)

Small amount of contrasting double-knitting-weight yarn iCord bows (optional)

Two stitch markers and stitch holder

Two 1.5–2cm wooden buttons

TENSION:
13½ sts to 10cm (4in) measured over garter stitch using 6mm needles.

ABBREVIATIONS:
See either page 14 or the inside back-cover flap.

TO MAKE THE LEFT SLIPPER
Using 6mm needles and main colour, cast on 61 sts.
Sole
Row 1 (RS): K61.
Row 2: K1, M1, K59, M1, K1. (63 sts)
Row 3: Knit.
Row 4: K1, M1, K61, M1, K1. (65 sts)
Work 8 rows in garter st (knit every row).
Upper
Row 1 (RS): K26, place marker (pm), K13, pm, K26.
Rows 2, 4 and 6: Purl.
Row 3: K24, SSK, slip marker (sm), K2tog, K9, SSK, sm, K2tog, K24. (61 sts)
Row 5: K23, SSK, sm, K2tog, K5, SSK, sm, K2tog, K23. (57 sts)
Row 7: K22, SSK, sm, K2tog, K1, SSK, sm, K2tog, K22. (53 sts)
Row 8: Knit.
Row 9 (RS): K10, cast off next 33 sts, K to end (10 sts now on needle after cast-off).**

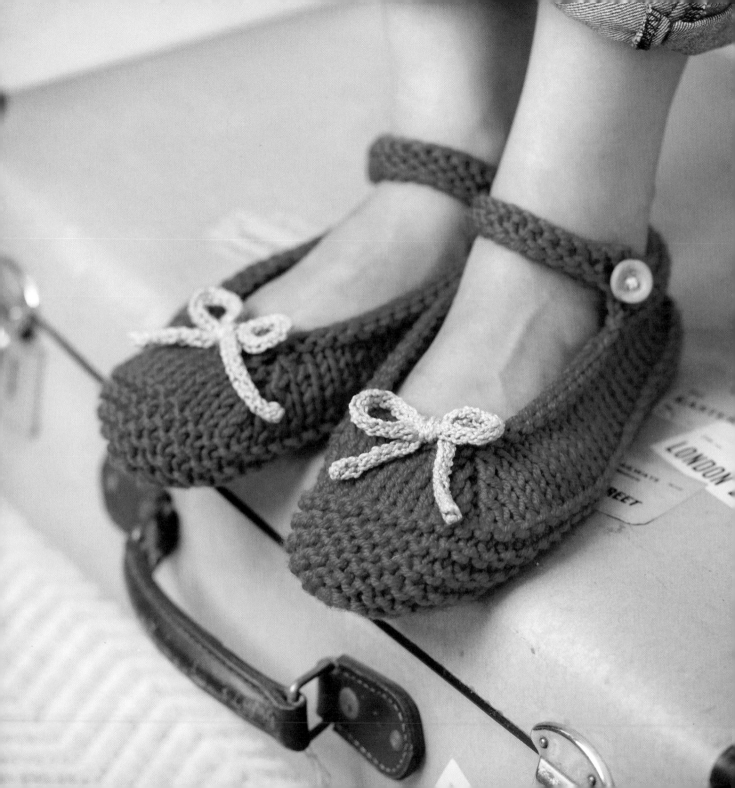

Strap

Row 1 (WS): K10, cast on 15 sts onto right needle with thumb method, slip remaining 10 sts onto a stitch holder. (25 sts)

Turn and cont on these 25 sts only.

Row 2: K25.

Row 3 (buttonhole): K23, yo, SSK.

Row 4: K25.

Cast off all 25 sts.

Return to sts on stitch holder and with WS facing, rejoin main colour and knit all 10 sts from stitch holder. Work 3 rows in garter stitch (knit every row).

Cast off.

TO MAKE THE RIGHT SLIPPER

Work as for Left Slipper to **.

Next row (WS): K10, slip remaining 10 sts onto a stitch holder.

Turn and cont on these 10 sts only. Work 3 rows in garter stitch (knit every row). Cast off.

Strap

Row 1 (WS): Using 6mm needles and main colour, cast on 15 sts onto right needle with thumb cast-on, then with same needle and WS facing knit all 10 sts from stitch holder. (25 sts)

Row 2: K25.

Row 3 (buttonhole): K2tog, yo, K23.

Row 4: K25.

Cast off all 25 sts.

TO SEW THE SEAMS

Fold the finished piece in half lengthways with right sides together, and sew the cast-on edges together with a simple whip stitch. Turn the slipper right side out so the right side is facing you and use garter stitch seam to sew the garter stitch sole of the heel. Insert the needle into the top loop of the stitch on one side and then in the bottom loop of the corresponding stitch on the other side (**1** and **2**). Continue alternating from side to side. When you reach the upper (st st) area of the slipper, switch to mattress stitch to complete the heel seam. Insert the needle under the horizontal bar between the first and second stitches and then under the bar on the corresponding stitch on the other side (**3** and **4**). Continue alternating from side to side.

TO FINISH

Sew a small button onto the outside edge of each slipper to correspond with the buttonhole.

If desired, use 4mm needles and contrasting DK yarn to make two 28cm 3-stitch i-cords for bows (see page 92). Tie in bows and sew one to front of of each slipper.

Weave in any stray yarn ends.

ribbed bobble hat

With wide ribbing and a folded brim, this hat is fantastically warm and snug. The classic bobble style means it's a great hat for both men and women to wear.

SIZE:
One size to fit women's small–medium

Length, unstretched: 26cm

Width, unstretched: 15.5cm

YARN:
Rowan *Wool Cotton DK*

Colour choices: Celedon (979) or Misty (903)

Amount: 2 x 50g balls for one hat

KNITTING NEEDLES & EXTRAS:
3.75mm circular knitting needle, 40cm long

Set of four 3.75mm double-pointed knitting needles

Stitch marker

TENSION:
22 sts and 30 rows to 10cm (4in) measured over st st using 3.75mm needles.

ABBREVIATIONS:
See either page 14 or the inside back-cover flap.

TO MAKE THE HAT
Using circular needle and chosen colour, cast on 108 sts.
Place a marker at beg of round and join for working in the round, being careful no stitches are twisted.
Round 1: *K2, P2; rep from * to end.
Repeat last round until your work measures 21cm from cast-on edge.
Shape crown
Once knitting becomes too tight for circular needle, transfer it evenly onto three double-pointed needles and knit with the fourth needle.
Round 1: *K2, P2tog, [K2, P2] twice; rep from * to end. (99 sts)

Round 2: *K2, P1, [K2, P2] twice; rep from * to end.

Round 3: Rep round 2.

Round 4: *K1, SSK, [K2, P2] twice; rep from * to end. (90 sts)

Round 5: *K4, P2, K2, P2; rep from * to end.

Round 6: Rep round 5.

Round 7: *K1, K2tog, K1, P2, K2, P2; rep from * to end. (81 sts)

Round 8: *K3, P2, K2, P2; rep from * to end.

Round 9: Rep round 8.

Round 10: *K1, K2tog, P2, K2, P2; rep from * to end. (72 sts)

Round 11: *K2, P2; rep from * to end.

Round 12: Rep round 11.

Round 13: *K2tog, P2, K2, P2; rep from * to end. (63 sts)

Round 14: *K1, P2, K2, P2; rep from * to end.

Round 15: Rep round 14.

Round 16: *K1, P2tog, K2, P2tog; rep from * to end. (45 sts)

Round 17: *K1, P1, K2tog, P1; rep from * to end. (36 sts)

Cut off yarn, leaving a long yarn tail. Thread the yarn tail onto a yarn needle, pass the needle through the remaining live stitches, pull to draw closed and secure. Leave the yarn tail to use to sew the pompom to the top of the hat.

Make a giant pompom 7cm in diameter. Using the long yarn tail on the hat, sew the pompom to the centre of the top of the hat. Weaving in any stray yarn ends.

WORKING AN SSK DECREASE

To work the decreases called SSK, first slip 2 sts purlwise onto the right needle (**1** and **2**). Then insert the left needle into the fronts of the 2 slipped sts (**3**) and knit them together (**4**).

TECHNIQUES USED

Working in the round - see page 44
SSK decrease – see right
K2tog decrease – see pages 28–29
Making a pompom – see page 121

cosy mittens

You can't go wrong with a classic pair of mittens. Leave them plain or embellish them with a colourful embroidered pattern… or a cheeky critter. If you're prone to losing your mittens, plait, crochet or knit a long i-cord to thread through your jacket sleeves.

SUPPLIES

SIZE:
Length, unstretched: 23cm

Circumference: 18cm

YARN:
Erika Knight *Vintage Wool*

Main colours: Bambi (034) for light brown pair; or Gorgeous (033) for pink pair

Amount: 1 x 50g ball of main colour makes one pair of mittens

Decoration colours: For light brown pair, scraps of DK-weight in light brown, mid-brown and green, and scraps of Aran-weight yarn in mid-brown, white and black; for pink pair, scraps of Aran-weight yarn in pale pink, white, gold and charcoal

KNITTING NEEDLES & EXTRAS:
Set of four 5mm double-pointed knitting needles

Set of four 2.5mm double-pointed knitting needles

Pair of 4mm knitting needles

TENSION:
18 sts and 24 rows to 10cm (4in) measured over st st using 5mm needles.

ABBREVIATIONS:
See either page 14 or the inside back-cover flap.

TO MAKE THE MITTENS (BOTH ALIKE)
Using 5mm double-pointed needles and main colour, cast on 30 sts. Distribute sts evenly on three needles (10 sts on each needle). Place a marker at beg of round and join for working in the round, being careful no stitches are twisted.
Rib round 1: *K1, P1; rep from * to end.
Repeat last round until cuff measures 7cm from cast-on edge.
Begin thumb shaping
Round 1: M1, K14, slip marker (sm), M1L, K1, M1R, sm, K15. (33 sts)
Round 2 and all even rounds: Knit.
Round 3: K15, sm, M1L, K3, M1R, sm, K15. (35 sts)
Round 5: K15, sm, M1L, K5, M1R, sm, K15. (37 sts)

Round 7: K15, sm, M1L, K7, M1R, sm, K15. (39 sts)
Round 9: K15, sm, M1L, K9, M1R, sm, K15. (41 sts)
Round 11: K15, sm, M1L, K11, M1R, sm, K15. (43 sts)
Round 13: K15, sm, M1L, K13, M1R, sm, K15. (45 sts)

Begin hand
Round 1: K15, slip next 15 sts onto a stitch holder removing markers, K 15 remaining sts by rejoining work in the round. (15 thumb sts remain unworked while hand is knitted.)
Round 2: K30.
Cont knitting every round until mitten just covers your little finger when tried on.

Shape top of hand
Rearrange sts onto just two needles (15 sts on each), removing last stitch marker.
Round 1: *K1, SSK, K to within 3 sts of the end of needle, K2tog, K1; rep from * to end of round.
Round 2: Knit.
Rounds 3–6: [Rep rounds 1 and 2] twice. (18 sts)
Round 7: Rep round 1. (14 sts)
There are now 6 sts on each needle, simply graft the sts together with kitchener stitch to finish the hand.

Complete thumb
Using 5mm double-pointed needles, distribute 15 thumb stitches evenly on three needles (5 sts on each needle) and with RS facing, join for working in round.
Using main colour, knit every round until work covers all but the very tip

of your thumb when tried on.
Shape top of thumb
Round 1: *K3, K2tog; rep from * to end of round. (12 sts)
Round 2: Knit.
Round 3: *K2, K2tog; rep from * to end of round. (9 sts)
Round 4: Knit.
Round 5: *K1, K2tog; rep from * to end of round. (6 sts)
Cut off yarn, leaving a long yarn tail. Thread the yarn tail onto a yarn needle, pass the needle through the remaining live stitches, pull to draw closed and secure.
Weave in any stray yarn ends.

TO BLOCK THE MITTENS
Wet block the pair of mittens as explained on page 103, patting the wet mittens into shape on a towel and leaving them to dry.
Once the work is completely dry, work the embellishment of your choice, making the acorns and leaves for the light brown pair only.

TO MAKE THE ACORNS
Using a mid-brown DK-weight yarn and a set of 2.5mm double-pointed needles, cast on 4 sts. Distribute sts over three needles.
Round 1: [KFB] 4 times. (8 sts)
Round 2: Knit.
Round 3: [KFB, k1] 4 times. (12 sts)
Rounds 4, 5, 6, 7 and 8: Knit.
Round 9: Change to light brown DK-weight yarn, KFB in each st. (24 sts)

Redistribute sts evenly on three needles (8 sts on each needle).
Round 10: Purl.
Round 11: K1, P1; rep from * to end.
Round 12: Work in moss st and decrease as follows – [P1, K1] 3 times, P2tog; rep from * twice more. (21 sts)
Round 13: Work in moss st and decrease as follows – [K1, P1] twice, K1, P2tog; rep from * twice more. (18 sts)
Round 14: [P2tog] 9 times. (9 sts)
Stuff acorn with scraps of yarn.
Round 15: [P2tog] 4 times, P1. (5 sts)
Round 16: P1, P2tog twice. (3 sts)**
Knit a 30cm i-cord on these 3 sts (see page 92) and cast off.
Make a second acorn and i-cord in exactly the same way.
Then make two acorns as for first acorn to ** and finish as follows:
Round 17: P2tog and fasten off.
Thread an i-cord through the top of the ribbing on each mitten as shown. Sew a second acorn to the other end of each i-cord.

TO MAKE THE ACORN LEAVES
Using 4mm needles and green DK-weight yarn, cast on 3 sts.
Row 1: Knit.
Row 2 and all even rows: Knit.
Row 3: KFB, P1, KFB. (5 sts)
Row 5: KFB, K1, P1, K1, KFB. (7 sts)

Row 7: KFB, K2, P1, K2, KFB. (9 sts)
Row 9: K2tog, K2, P1, K2, K2tog. (7 sts)
Row 11: K2tog, K1, P1, K1, K2tog. (5 sts)
Row 13: Rep row 5. (7 sts)
Row 15: Rep row 7. (9 sts)
Row 17: KFB, K3, P1, K3, KFB. (11 sts)
Row 19: K2tog, K3, P1, K3, K2tog. (9 sts)
Row 21: Rep row 9. (7 sts)
Row 23: Rep row 7. (9 sts)
Row 25: Rep row 17. (11 sts)
Row 27: KFB, K4, P1, K4, KFB. (13 sts)
Row 29: KFB, K5, P1, K5, KFB. (15 sts)
Row 31: K2tog, K5, P1, K5, K2tog. (13 sts)
Row 33: K2tog, K4, P1, K4, K2tog. (11 sts)
Row 34: K2tog, K to last 2 sts, K2tog. (9 sts)

Row 35: K2tog, K2, P1, K2, K2tog. (7 sts)
Row 37: KFB, K2, P1, K2, KFB. (9 sts)
Row 39: K3, turn work, K3, turn work, K2tog, K1, turn work, K2tog and fasten off.
Rejoin yarn to RS, K1, P1, K1, turn work, K3, turn work, K1, P1, K1, turn work, K2tog, K1, turn work, K2tog and fasten off.
Rejoin yarn to RS, K3, turn work, K3, turn work, K2tog, K1, turn work, K2tog and fasten off.
Make three more leaves in the same way and sew two to each acorn.

TECHNIQUES USED

Working in the round –
see page 44
SSK decrease –
see page 52
K2tog decrease –
see pages 28–29
KFB increase –
see pages 32–33
Duplicate stitch –
see page 104

IMPORTANT NOTE

The duplicate-stitch squirrel is actually worked upside down on the mittens, so turn the chart around by 180° when embroidering the motif.

KEY

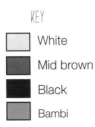

- ☐ White
- ▨ Mid brown
- ■ Black
- ▨ Bambi

TO EMBROIDER THE MITTENS

To work the squirrel in duplicate stitch on the light brown pair, follow the chart below, centering the squirrel on the front of each mitten and reversing one to face in the opposite direction, if preferred.
To work the embroidery on the pink pair, embroider three stripes of duplicate stitch across the front 15 stitches of the mittens only, working the first row 4 rows above the ribbing and the other two 5 rows apart. Use white, pink, gold and grey yarns alternately for the stitches across the stripe. Work five French knots between the embroidered stripes as shown.

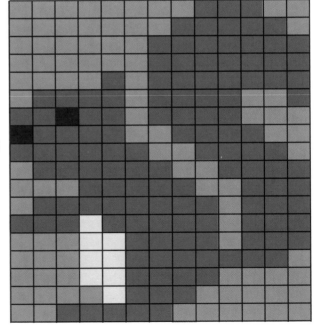

WHETHER YOU LOVE CUTE WOODLAND CRITTERS OR
COLOURFUL POLKA DOTS, CUSTOMISE YOUR MITTENS
TO MAKE THEM UNIQUE

moss stitch cowl

There is nothing better than a big, squishy cowl to keep you warm, no? This pattern uses a gorgeous super-chunky yarn and a dense moss stitch. Just keep going until you run out of yarn – the bigger the better, I say.

SUPPLIES

SIZE:
Circumference: 111cm

Width: 23cm

YARN:
Erika Knight *Maxi Wool*

Colour: Artisan (020)

Amount: 2 x 100g balls

KNITTING NEEDLES & EXTRAS:
10mm circular knitting needle, 40cm long

Stitch marker

TECHNIQUES USED
Working in the round – see page 44
Moss stitch – see right

TENSION:
9 sts and 17½ rows to 10cm (4in) measured over moss stitch pattern using 10mm needles.

ABBREVIATIONS:
See either page 14 or the inside back-cover flap.

TO MAKE THE COWL
Cast on 100 sts.
Place a marker at beg of round and join for working in the round, being careful no stitches are twisted.
Round 1: *K1, P1; rep from * to end.
Round 2: *P1, K1; rep from * to end.
Last two rounds are repeated to form moss st pattern.
Cont in moss st until your work measures approximately 23cm from cast-on edge, or until you run out of yarn. The chunkier the better, I say!
Cast off knitwise.

TO FINISH
Weave in any stray yarn ends.
Do not press.

WORKING MOSS STITCH
Whilst working moss stitch, when you change from a knit to a purl stitch, you must be sure that the yarn is in the correct position to work the next stitch.
When knitting a stitch the yarn is always held at the back of the work and when purling a stitch the yarn is always held at the front of the work.

diamond leg warmers

Knitted in a scrumptious, textured diamond pattern using only knit and purl stitches, these leg warmers are fantastic when you need that extra bit of comfort inside a pair of wellies or some snuggly warmth on a winter's day.

SIZE:
Circumference, unstretched: 24cm

Width, unstretched: 12cm

Length: 30cm

YARN
Rico *Essentials Soft Merino Aran*

Colour: Mandarin (070)

Amount: 2 x 50g balls

KNITTING NEEDLES & EXTRAS:
Set of four 5mm double-pointed knitting needles

Stitch marker

TENSION:
17 sts and 24 rows to 10cm (4in) measured over diamond stitch pattern using 5mm needles.

ABBREVIATIONS:
See either page 14 or the inside back-cover flap.

TO MAKE THE LEG WARMERS

Cast on 40 sts.

Distribute sts onto three double-pointed needles (13 on needle one, 13 on needle two, 14 on needle three).

Place a marker at beg of round and join for working in the round, being careful no stitches are twisted.

Rib round 1: *K1, P1; rep from * to end.

Repeat last round 5 times more. (A total of 6 rib rounds have been worked.)

Next round: *K1, P1; rep from * to end, M1. (41 sts)

Begin diamond pattern

Round 1: K4, [P1, K7] 4 times (5 sts remain), P1, K4.

Round 2: K3, [P1, K1, P1, K5] 4 times (6 sts remain), P1, K1, P1, K3.

Round 3: K2, [P1, K3] 9 times (3 sts remain), P1, K2.

Round 4: K1, *P1, K5, P1, K1; rep from * to end.

Round 5: [P1, K7] 5 times (1 st remains), P1.

Round 6: Rep round 4.

Round 7: Rep round 3.

Round 8: Rep round 2.

Rounds 1–8 are repeated to form the pattern.

[Repeat rounds 1–8] 6 times more. (A total of seven 8-round pattern repeats have been worked.)

Repeat pattern round 1 once more to complete the pattern.

Next round: K2tog, P1, *K1, P1; rep from * to end.

Next round: *K1, P1; rep from * to end.

Repeat last round 5 times more.

Cast off in rib.

Make a second leg warmer in the same way.

TO FINISH

Weave in any stray yarn ends.

TO SPRAY BLOCK THE LEG WARMERS

To really bring this stitch pattern to life, it is essential that you spray block the knitting.

Lay out a clean, dry bath towel on a flat surface. Place each leg warmer on this towel and pin evenly to a width of 12cm and a length of 30cm. Using a spray bottle filled with water, spritz the knitting until wet through.

Leave the legwarmers to dry overnight.

TECHNIQUES USED

Knit stitch –
see pages 22–23
Purl stitch –
see pages 24–25
M1 increase –
see pages 34–35
K2tog decrease –
see pages 28–29
Wet blocking –
see right

winter cape

Reminiscent of a traditional raglan sweater, this super-soft cape is knitted from the top down on circular needles and shaped with basic increases. A great starting point if you want to slowly graduate to the world of sweater knitting.

SUPPLIES

SIZE:
Length from top of shoulder to bottom edge of cape: 47cm

Circumference around bottom edge of cape: 113cm

Turtleneck, unstretched: length 20cm, width 20cm, circumference 40cm

YARN
Rico *Creative Twist Super Chunky*

Colour: Charcoal (05)

Amount: 4 x 100g balls

KNITTING NEEDLES & EXTRAS:
10mm circular knitting needle, 40cm long

10mm circular knitting needle, 80cm long

10mm circular knitting needle, 100cm long

Four stitch markers

TENSION:
8½ sts and 12 rows to 10cm (4in) measured over st st using 10mm needles.

ABBREVIATIONS:
See either page 14 or the inside back-cover flap.

TECHNIQUES USED

Working in the round – see page 44
K1, P1 ribbing – see page 68
KFB increase – see pages 32–33
Spray blocking – see page 65

TO MAKE THE CAPE

Using 40cm-long circular needle, cast on 40 sts.

Place a marker at beg of round and join for working in the round, being careful no stitches are twisted.

Turtleneck

The cape is begun at the top of the turtleneck.

Rib round 1: *K1, P1; rep from * to end.

Repeat last round 21 times more, placing a marker after every 10 sts on last rib round. (It is a good idea to use different colour markers than the one used at the beginning of the round, so you can keep track of your rounds easily.)

Shape shoulders

As you continue to increase stitches at the shoulders, your work will grow and, at various stages, you will need to transfer your stitches onto the longer circular needles. By the time you finish increasing you should be using the 100cm circular needle. Begin increasing as follows:

Round 1: KFB, [K to within 1 st of marker, KFB, sm, KFB] 3 times, K to last st at end of round, KFB.
(8 sts increased in round)

Round 2: Knit.

Repeat last two rounds 6 times more. (96 sts)

Work in st st (knit every round) without shaping for 38 rounds more (approximately 32cm more).

Next round: *K1, P1; rep from * to end.

Repeat last round 4 times more. Cast off knitwise.

TO FINISH

Weave in any stray yarn ends. Spray block cape on a flat surface, paying particular attention to the increase seams at the shoulder and leave to dry overnight. This will encourage a lovely, silky drape when the cape is worn.

WORKING KNIT ONE, PURL ONE RIB

When knitting a stitch the yarn is always held at the back of the work (**1**) and when purling a stitch the yarn is always held at the front of the work (**2**).

Whilst working any rib stitch, when you change from a knit to a purl stitch, you must be sure that the yarn is in the correct position to work the next stitch.

When you are moving the yarn from the back to the front, or from the front to the back, the yarn should go between the two needle rather than over them.

knits to share

- Maiden braid bracelet • Bow necklace
- iPhone case • Cable headband
- Coin purse • Pompom necklace
- Bow-wow bow tie

maiden braid bracelet

Simply a stand-alone cable braid, these bangles remind me of oversized friendship bracelets. If you are new to knitting cables, these bracelets are fantastic practise pieces.

SIZE:

Circumference around outside of bracelet: 22.5cm

Width: 2.5cm

Note: Bracelet circumference is adjustable.

YARN:

King Cole *Bamboo Cotton DK*

Main colour choices: Pebble (610) or Yellow (523)

Amount: Approximately 20g for each bracelet

KNITTING NEEDLES & EXTRAS:

Pair of 3.75mm knitting needles

Extra knitting needle for three-needle cast-off (3.75mm or smaller)

4mm crochet hook

Cable needle

Small amount of scrap yarn in a contrasting colour for provisional cast-on

TENSION:

It is not necessary to work this bracelet to an exact tension.

ABBREVIATIONS:

C12F slip 6 sts onto cable needle and hold at front of work, knit next 6 sts, then knit 6 sts from cable needle.

C12B slip 6 sts onto cable needle and hold at back of work, knit next 6 sts, then knit 6 sts from cable needle.

See also either page 14 or the inside back-cover flap.

TECHNIQUES USED

Provisional crochet-chain cast-on or open cast-on - see page 74
Picking up stitches
Front and back cables
Three-needle cast-off

73

TO MAKE THE BRACELET

Using a crochet hook and contrasting scrap yarn, make 18 chain and fasten off. Using knitting needles and main colour yarn, pick up and knit one st in each of the chain sts. (18 sts)

Alternatively, cast on 18 sts using the open cast-on method (see right). Begin cable pattern as follows:

Row 1: K18.
Row 2: P18.
Row 3: C12F, K6.
Row 4: P18.
Row 5: K18.
Row 6: P18.
Row 7: K6, C12B.
Row 8: P18.
Row 9: K18.
Row 10: P18.

[Repeat rows 3–10] 6 times more, then work rows 3–8 only for the last (eighth) repeat.

Set aside – do not cast off and do not cut off yarn.

TO ADJUST THE LENGTH

For a longer (or shorter) bracelet, alter the number of cable repeats. Make sure you work only cable rows 3–8 for the last repeat. This ensures the braid is continuously joined.

TO FINISH

Join the ends of the bracelet together with the three-needle cast-off (see right).

Weave in any stray yarn ends and turn the bracelet right side out.

WORKING THE THREE-NEEDLE CAST-OFF

With the right side of the work facing you and the cast-on edge at the top, work from right to left and slip each picked-up stitch from the crochet chain onto an extra knitting needle, being careful not to split the fibres. Find that knotted end of the chain and undo the very last stitch – you should be able to pull gently on the tail and watch the chain unzip neatly. (I find this very satisfying!) You will see you have the same number of live stitches at either end of the knitting. Bring the two needles together so that the right sides of the knitting are together and the wrong sides are facing outwards. Hold the two needles in the left hand ready to start the cast-off. This cast-off method leaves a ridge, but it will be hidden on the inside. Using a third needle, cast off all stitches in the usual way but inserting the right needle through one stitch on each left needle as you cast-off.

WORKING THE OPEN CAST-ON

Cut a strand of contrast yarn. With the working yarn, make a slip knot and place on two needles (**1**). Hold the waste yarn beside the slip knot and take the working yarn under it and over the needles from front to back. Bring the working yarn in front of the waste yarn (**2**). Repeat step 2 until all the stitches are cast on (**3**). Take out one needle before knitting the first row (**4**). Remove the waste yarn only when you are ready to pick up stitches along this cast-on edge.

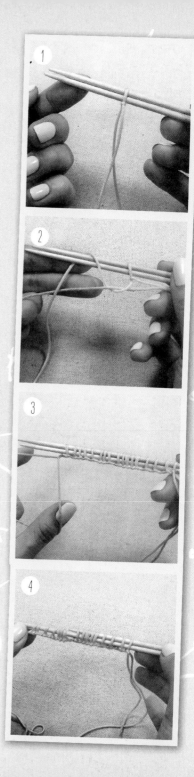

bow necklace

These bow necklaces were one of the first knits I ever designed. They are delicate and oh-so cute. As well as adding them to a necklace chain, try attaching them to other jewellery findings, such as a brooch pin or a ring blank, to create a whole set.

SUPPLIES

SIZE:
Across finished bow: 4cm

Bow width: 2.5cm

YARN:
Sirdar *Snuggly Baby Bamboo DK*

Colour choices: Light Blue (169), Shrimpy (119) or Perky Pink (124)

King Cole *Bamboo Cotton DK*

Colour choice: Mint (517)

Amount: Approximately 5g for one bow

KNITTING NEEDLES & EXTRAS:
Pair of 3.75mm knitting needles

46cm-long necklace chain with clasp

Two 4mm jump rings

Two pairs of slim jewellery pliers

TENSION:
It is not necessary to work the bow to an exact tension.

ABBREVIATIONS:
See either page 14 or the inside back-cover flap.

TO MAKE THE BOW
Using chosen colour, cast on 18 sts.

Work 10 rows in garter stitch (knit every row).

Cast off, leaving a long yarn tail. Thread the yarn tail onto a yarn needle. Bring the two side edges together and sew the seam using the garter stitch seam method (see page 49).

Weave in any stray yarn ends.

Fold the bow with the seam at the centre back.

Pinch the centre of the bow together and firmly wrap a long length of yarn several times around the middle.

Tie a double knot to secure and weave in the yarn ends.

TO ASSEMBLE THE NECKLACE
Using two pairs of slim jewellery pliers, open the jump rings and loop them onto a stitch halfway up the inside of each side of the bow, without closing shut. Lay the necklace chain through the jump ring on one side, and close it. Pass one end of the chain through the center wrap of the bow and pull it through gently until the lengths of chain are even. Lay the chain through the remaining open jump ring and close it to secure.

iphone case

This case really has it all, aside from protecting your phone from bumps and scratches, it has a protective strap to hold the phone in place and a nifty pocket to stash your cards and cash. What more could you need?

SIZE:
Width, unstretched: 6.5cm

Length: 12.5cm (adjustable)

YARN:
Rico *Essentials Merino DK*

Colour choices: Natural (60) and Wood (53) for white and brown case; or Natural (60) and Yellow (65) for white and yellow case

Amounts: 1 x 50g ball in Wood or Yellow and a small amount in Natural

KNITTING NEEDLES & EXTRAS:
Set of four 3.75mm double-pointed knitting needles

Stitch marker

3.5mm crochet hook

1.5cm button

TENSION:
24 sts and 34 rows to 10cm (4in) measured over st st using 3.75mm needles.

ABBREVIATIONS:
See either page 14 or the inside back-cover flap.

TO MAKE THE CASE
Using knitting needles and Natural, cast on 32 sts. Distribute sts evenly on three needles (8 sts on each needle). Place a marker at beg of round and join for working in the round, being careful no stitches are twisted.

Rib round 1: *K1, P1; rep from * to end.

Repeat last round until ribbing

TECHNIQUES USED
Three-needle cast-off
Picking up and knitting stitches on st st –
see page 81
Mattress stitch –
see page 49
Crochet chain

measures 2cm from cast-on edge. Change to Wood or Yellow and work in st st (knit every round) for a further 10.5cm, or until knitting covers your device.

Cut off yarn, leaving a very long length of yarn for casting off.

Turn knitting wrong side out. With the working yarn at the tip of one of the needles, re-distribute the sts onto two knitting needles (16 sts on each needle).

Bring the two needles together so that the right sides of the knitting are together and the wrong sides are facing outwards. Hold the two needles in the left hand ready to start the cast-off.

Using a third needle, cast off all stitches in the usual way but inserting the right needle through one stitch on each left needle as you cast off.

Turn the case right side out.

TO MAKE THE POCKET

Decide which side of the case you want the pocket on. There are 16 sts across each side of the case and you will be picking up 14 sts across the case, so start picking up the stitches one stitch in from the right side-edge at the bottom of the case – and one row up from the seam. When picking up the stitches hold the case with the ribbing at the top. To pick up the first stitch, insert a 3.75mm knitting needle between the two legs of the V-shaped stitch and pick up the horizontal bar, wrap the yarn (Yellow or Wood) around the needle and pull the working yarn through (**1**). Working horizontally across the bottom of the case, pick up and knit one stitch in each of the next 13 stitches. (14 sts) (**2**) Beg with a purl row, work in st st (working one purl row and one knit row alternately) until the pocket measures 7cm, ending with a purl (WS) row (**3**).

Next row: [K1, P1] to end.

Repeat last row 3 times more.

Cast off.

Align the edge of the pocket flap with the adjacent column of stitches on the case and use mattress stitch to invisibly join the two pieces. Repeat this on both sides of the pocket.

Weave in any stray yarn ends.

TO MAKE THE STRAP

Sew the button to the pocket just below the ribbing.

Using crochet hook and Natural, insert the hook around the centre stitch at the bottom of the ribbing, wrap the yarn around the hook and pull a loop through. Work 40 chain stitches or until the chain reaches the top of the case, down around the button and back to the beginning of the chain. Fasten off and sew to the end of the first chain. Weave in any stray yarn ends.

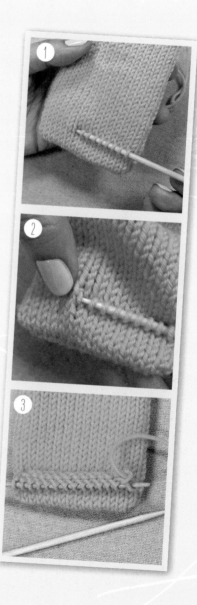

cable headband

Perfect for keeping your ears warm without ruining your 'do, this delightful twistedcable headband is knitted flat and then grafted together with an invisible seam.

SUPPLIES

SIZE:

Circumference, unstretched: 47cm

Width: 10cm

Note: Headband circumference is adjustable.

YARN:

Rico *Essentials Big*

Colour: Coral (017)

Amount: 1 x 50g ball

KNITTING NEEDLES & EXTRAS:

Pair of 8mm knitting needles

8mm crochet hook

Cable needle

Small amount of scrap yarn in a contrasting colour for provisional cast-on

TENSION:

It is not necessary to work this headband to an exact tension.

ABBREVIATIONS:

C12F slip 6 sts onto cable needle and hold at front of work, knit next 6 sts, then knit 6 sts from cable needle.

C12B slip 6 sts onto cable needle and hold at back of work, knit next 6 sts, then knit 6 sts from cable needle.

See also either page 14 or the inside back-cover flap.

TO MAKE THE HEADBAND

Using crochet hook and contrasting scrap yarn, make 18 chain and fasten off. Using knitting needles and main colour, pick up and knit one st in each of the chain sts. (18 sts)

Row 1: K18.

Row 2: P18.

Continue working in st st until work measures 16cm from cast-on edge.

Cable pattern

Begin 8-row cable pattern as follows:

Row 1: C12F, K6.

Rows 2, 4, 6 and 8: P18.

Rows 3 and 7: K18.

Row 5: K6, C12B.

Repeat cable pattern rows 1–8 twice more.

Beg with a K row, work in st st (knit one row, purl one row alternately) for 16cm.

If necessary, adjust length of headband before cutting off yarn.

Do not cast off.

Cut off yarn, leaving a long yarn tail to work the kitchener stitch seam.

TO GRAFT THE ENDS TOGETHER

With the right side of the knitting facing you and the cast-on edge at the top, work from right to left and slip each picked up stitches from the crochet chain onto an extra knitting needle and remove the waste yarn. You will see you have the same number of live stitches at either end of the knitting.

TO WORK THE KITCHENER STITCH SEAM

Thread a blunt-ended needle with the long yarn tail. Hold the two knitting needles together parallel, with wrong sides facing, and the needle from which the long tail comes at the back. * Insert the needle purlwise into the first stitch on the front knitting needle (**1**). Pull the yarn through, leaving the stitch on the knitting needle. Insert the needle knitwise into the first stitch on the back knitting needle (**2**). Pull the yarn through, leaving the stitch on the knitting needle. Insert the needle knitwise into the first stitch on the front needle (**3**). Slip the stitch off the needle. Insert the needle purlwise into the next stitch on the front needle (**4**). Pull the yarn through, leaving the stitch on the needle. Insert the needle purlwise into the first stitch on the back needle (**5**). Slip the stitch off the needle. Insert the needle knitwise into the next stitch on the back needle. Pull the yarn through, leaving the stitch on the needle. Repeat from * until all the stitches have been grafted (**6** and **7**). Weave in any stray yarn ends.

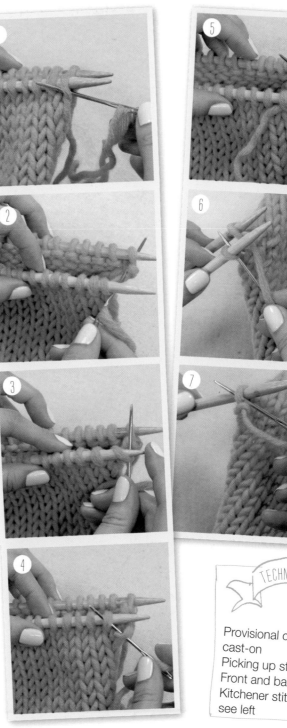

TECHNIQUES USED

Provisional crochet-chain cast-on
Picking up stitches
Front and back cables
Kitchener stitch seam – see left

coin purse

When I was eight years old my Grandma gave me a coin purse just like this one, which I carried everywhere. It's the prettiest pouch for your loose change and the knitted lining makes it extra strong and durable.

SUPPLIES

SIZE:

Width across top: 7.5cm

Length from top edge to base: 7cm

YARN:

Erika Knight *Blue Wool*

Colours: Iced Gem (041) and Milk (036)

Amounts: 1 x 26g ball of each colour

KNITTING NEEDLES & EXTRAS:

Set of five 4mm double-pointed knitting needles

Stitch marker

Stitch holder

7.5cm metal coin purse frame

Fabric glue and toothpicks

TENSION:

22 sts and 30 rows to 10cm (4in) measured over st st using 4mm needles.

ABBREVIATIONS:

See either page 14 or the inside back-cover flap.

TO MAKE THE PURSE

Using Iced Gem and double-pointed needles, cast on 15 sts onto one needle.

Purse base

Using two needles and beg with a K row, work 7 rows in st st (knit one row, purl one row alternately), so ending with a K row.

Purse sides

Leave the sts on your needle and use three new needles to pick up and knit 7 sts along one side edge, 15 sts along the cast-on edge and 7 sts along the other side. (44 sts) Place a marker at beg of round and join for working in the round, taking care no stitches are twisted.

Work in st st (knit every round) until your purse measures 4cm from pick-up round.

Next round: K17, K2tog, K20, K2tog, leaving the last 3 sts unworked. (42 sts)

Shape top of purse

Re-arrange your sts onto just two needles – slip the last 3 unworked sts and next 18 sts onto one needle and slip remaining 21 sts onto a stitch holder.

**Work back and forth in rows on the 21 sts on the needle as follows:
Row 1 (RS): SSK, K to last 2 sts, K2tog. (19 sts)
Purl 1 row, K 1 row, purl 1 row.
Row 5: SSK, K to last 2 sts, K2tog. (17 sts)
Purl 1 row.
Row 7: SSK, K to last 2 sts, K2tog. (15 sts)
Do not cast off. Cut off yarn, leaving sts on a spare needle.**
Return to sts on holder, and with RS facing, rejoin yarn and work as first side from ** to **.

TO MAKE THE LINING
Using Milk and double-pointed needles, cast on 13 sts.
Lining base
Using two needles and beg with a K row, work 5 rows in st st, so ending with a K row.
Lining sides
Leave the sts on your needle and use three new needles to pick up and knit 6 sts along one side edge, 13 sts along the cast-on edge and 6 sts along the other side. (38 sts)
Place a marker at beg of round and join in the round.
Work in st st (knit every round) until your lining measures 4cm from pick-up round.
Next round: K35, leaving the last 3 sts unworked.

Shape top of lining
Re-arrange your sts onto just two needles – slip the last 3 unworked sts and next 16 sts onto one needle and slip remaining 19 sts onto a stitch holder.

***Work back and forth in rows on the 19 sts on the needle as follows:
Row 1 (RS): SSK, K to last 2 sts, K2tog. (17 sts)
Purl 1 row, K 1 row, purl 1 row.
Row 5: SSK, K to last 2 sts, K2tog. (15 sts)
Purl 1 row.
Do not cast off. Cut off yarn, leaving sts on needle.***
Return to sts on holder, and with RS facing, rejoin yarn and work as first side from *** to ***.

TO JOIN THE PURSE AND THE LINING
Turn the lining inside out and arrange it inside the purse piece.

Slip the sts of each side of purse onto a double-pointed needle. Hold purse and lining sts on one side together with purse side facing you. Using a third needle and Iced Gem, cast off in the usual way but inserting right needle through one st on each left needle as you cast off. Use the yarn tails of your cast-off to sew the side edges together.
Use the three-needle cast-off to join the other side in the same way.
Weave in any remaining ends.
Using a toothpick, spread the fabric glue into the space of one side of the purse frame, so the whole surface is covered. Gently maneuver one side of the purse into the frame from one end to the other, using a clean toothpick to push the edges as far as they will go. Leave the glue to dry for the required time before attaching the other side.

pompom necklace

Inspired by a pompom garland I made to brighten up my work studio, this necklace adds a big helping of whimsy to your outfit. Make the pompoms as big as you dare!

SUPPLIES

SIZE:
Circumference of necklace: 70cm

Pompom: 4cm in diameter

YARN:
Debbie Bliss *Cashmerino Aran*

Colours: Charcoal (028), White (025) and Kingfisher (062)

Amount: Approximately 20g of each colour

KNITTING NEEDLES & EXTRAS:
Two 3.75mm double-pointed knitting needles

2cm pompom maker or cardboard to make templates

TENSION:
It is not necessary to work the i-cord chain to an exact tension.

ABBREVIATIONS:
See either page 14 or the inside back-cover flap.

TECHNIQUES USED

Knitting an i-cord – see page 92
Making pompoms – see page 121

TO MAKE THE NECKLACE CHAIN

Using Charcoal, cast on 3 sts onto one double-pointed needle (**1**). Use a second double-pointed needle to knit the i-cord as follows:

Round 1: K3.

Round 2: Without turning your work, slide all 3 stitches to the opposite end of your needle, pass the working yarn behind the stitches and K3 (**2**).

Repeat last round until your i-cord measures 40cm (**3**).

Cast off, leaving a 30cm yarn tail. Weave in the short yarn tail at the cast-on end of the i-cord.

TO MAKE THE POMPOMS

Using a pompom maker, make two 4cm pompoms in Charcoal, three in White and two in Kingfisher. If you do not have a pompom maker, make the pompoms with two cardboard rings (see page 121). To make really dense, fluffy pompoms, wrap the yarn around lots of times before you tie and cut them. Trim carefully with sharp embroidery scissors to even up the edges.

TO ASSEMBLE THE NECKLACE

To bring your necklace to life, thread the long yarn tail on your iCord through a yarn needle and carefully pass it through the center of a Charcoal pompom, a White pompom, a Kingfisher pompom, a White pompom, a Kingfisher pompom, a White pompom and a Charcoal pompom. Now take the opposite end of your iCord and thread the yarn tail through its centre for around 10-15cm, pulling the pompoms as close as possible to the end of the i-cord. Weave the yarn tail into the i-cord to secure it.

bow-wow bow tie

Not just for dogs, this dapper bow tie will add some serious suave to any neckline. There is some very basic sewing involved, but if I can do it, you can do it too!

SIZE:
Across finished bow: 14cm

Bow width: 7cm

Strap circumference: Adjustable

YARN:
Sirdar *Flirt DK*

Colour: Mesmerise (216)

Amount: 1 x 50g

KNITTING NEEDLES & EXTRAS:
Pair of 4mm knitting needles

38cm length of 2cm black elastic

Bow tie 'hook and eye' fastening

Sewing needle and black cotton sewing thread

TENSION:
It is not necessary to work the bow to an exact tension.

ABBREVIATIONS:
See either page 14 or the inside back-cover flap.

TO MAKE THE BOW
Cast on 60 sts.
Work 30 rows in garter stitch (knit every row).
Cast off, leaving a 30cm yarn tail.
Thread the long yarn tail onto a blunt-tipped yarn needle. Fold the knitting in half lengthways and sew the short side edges together.
Weave in any stray yarn ends.

TO MAKE THE BOW-TIE CENTRE
Cast on 10 sts.
Beg with a K row, work 14 rows in st st (knit one row, purl one row alternately).
Cast off, leaving a 30cm yarn tail.
Thread the long yarn tail onto a blunt-tipped yarn needle. Sew the cast-on edge to the cast-off edge using basic whip stitch.
Weave in any stray yarn ends.

TO ASSEMBLE THE COLLAR

Fold the bow piece in half with the right sides together and the seam at the centre back. Pass the bow through the centre piece, unfolding as you proceed, and manipulate it into a traditional bow shape.

Feed the length of black elastic through the back of the bow centre. Slip one end of the elastic strap through the hook section of the fastenings, with the hook facing outwards, and sew it back to the strap using a sewing needle and black thread. Thread the other end through the adjustor section first, facing outwards, then through the eye section. pulling it long and doubling back through the back of the adjustor section. Fold the raw edge of the elastic back on itself and sew in place to secure.

TECHNIQUES USED

Garter stitch
Stocking stitch
Whip stitch – see right

OTHER IDEAS

WHY NOT TRY ADDING THIS KNITTED BOW TO A HEADBAND TO MAKE A CUTE HAIR BOW, OR LOOP IT OVER A BELT TO ACCESSORISE AN OUTFIT.

TO WORK THE WHIP STITCH SEAM

Place the knitted piece with wrong sides together (**1**). Thread a blunt-ended needle with the long tail of yarn. Insert the yarn needle through the front edge, taking it through the back edge at a diagonal angle (**2**). Continue passing the needle through both front and back edges at a diagonal until the seam is sewn (**3**). Weave in any stray yarn ends.

knits for your home

- Flamingo cushion • Triangle motif throw
- Cotton dishcloth • Chevron cushion
- Egg cosy caps • Hedgehog paperweight

flamingo cushion

Flamingos, I hear, get their pink colour from the algae they eat in their natural watery habitat. This fine feathery friend is stitched to the cushion after it has been knitted, using duplicate stitch. No algae needed!

SUPPLIES

SIZE:
Width: 40cm

Length: 40cm

YARN:
Debbie Bliss *Cashmerino Aran*

Colours: Grey (009), Rose (053), White (025) and Black (300)

Amounts: 3 x 50g balls in Grey, 1 x 50g ball in Rose, and a small amount each in White and Black

KNITTING NEEDLES & EXTRAS:
Pair of 5mm knitting needles

Three 3.5cm buttons

40cm x 40cm cushion pad

TENSION:
18 sts and 24 rows to 10cm (4in) measured over st st using 5mm needles.

ABBREVIATIONS:
See either page 14 or the inside back-cover flap.

SPECIAL NOTE:
The cushion cover is worked in stocking stitch with a ribbed border along the edges of the back opening. Once the cushion has been completed the flamingo is worked in duplicate stitch, also known as Swiss darning.

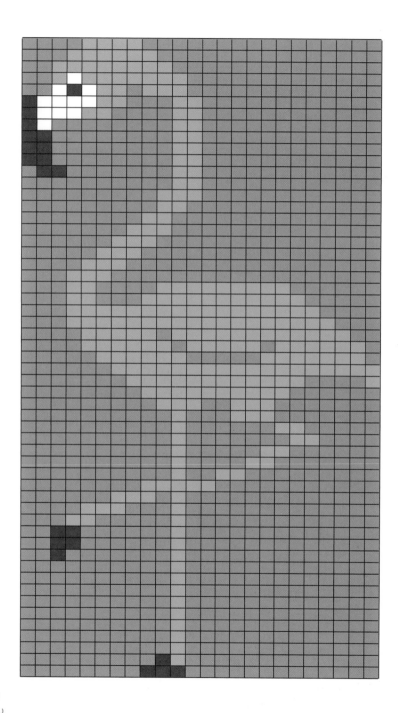

TO MAKE THE CUSHION COVER

Using Grey, cast on 72 sts.
Begin K1, P1 ribbing as follows:
Rib row 1: *K1, P1; rep from * to end.
Repeat last row 8 times more. (A total of 9 rib rows have been worked.)
Beg working in st st as follows:
Row 1 (RS): Knit.
Row 2: Purl.
Repeat last 2 rows until your work measures 80cm from the cast-on edge, ending with a purl (WS) row.
Next row (RS): *K1, P1; rep from * to end.
Work 3 rows more in K1, P1 ribbing as set, so ending with a WS row.
Buttonholes
Keeping the rib correct as set, work buttonholes over next 2 rows as follows (see page 103 for further explanation):
Buttonhole row 1 (RS): Rib 15 sts, cast off next 4 sts, *work in rib until there are 15 sts on right needle after last cast-off, cast off next 4 sts; rep from * once more, rib to end.
Buttonhole row 2: Keeping rib correct as set, *rib 15 sts, turn work, cast on 4 sts onto the left needle using the knit cast-on, turn work: rep from * twice more, rib to end.
Work 3 rows more in rib.
Cast off.

KEY

▨	Rose (053)
▨	Black (300)
▨	Grey (009)
□	White (025)

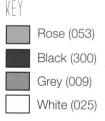

TO WORK THE BUTTONHOLES

On the first buttonhole row, work in rib to the position of the buttonhole and then cast off the next 4 stitches in the usual way (**1**, **2** and **3**).

Repeat these steps for each subequent buttonhole and then work in rib to the end of the row (**4**).

On the second buttonhole row, work in rib to the cast-off stitches and then cast on the same number of stitches using either the knit cast-on method (see pages 20–21) or the single cast-on method.

To work the single cast-on method, wrap the working yarn around your left thumb from front to back and secure it in your palm with your other fingers. Insert the needle upwards through the strand on your thumb (**5**). Slip this loop from your thumb onto the needle, pulling the yarn to tighten it (**6**).

If using the single cast-on method, on the next row knit into the back of the cast on stitches tighten them (**7**).

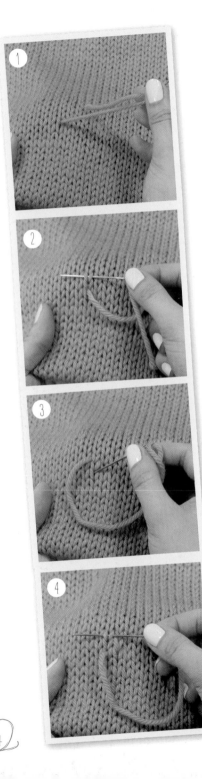

TO BLOCK THE CUSHION COVER

Weave in any stray yarn ends.
As stocking stitch curls at the edges, it is essential to wet block the cushion cover to the correct measurements before adding the flamingo. This helps to smooth out and set the stitches, creating a flawless fabric. Submerge the entire piece in a shallow bath of tepid water. Let it soak for a few minutes until wet through. Carefully lift it from the water supporting the entire weight, so as not to stretch it. Squeeze out excess water without wringing or twisting and place the knitting on a dry towel. Bring together the edges of the towel and press out as much moisture as possible. Now lay out a clean, dry bath towel on a flat surface. Place the knitting on this towel and pin it to a width of 40cm and a length of 84cm. Leave it to dry.

TO SEW THE SIDE SEAMS

Once the work is completely dry, wrap it right side out around the cushion pad with the ribbed edges overlapping. Pin the folded sides loosely to create a square, and mark where you will need to sew, ensuring the stitches line up with the corresponding row. Using mattress stitch, sew each side seam.

TO ADD THE FLAMINGO MOTIF

Make sure the button band is the correct way up before starting the colour chart. The full chart is 24 sts wide and 55 sts tall. You may like to use four lengths of scrap yarn to mark the boundaries as you position it centrally on the front of the cushion. Each square on the chart represents a stitch on the knitting. The flamingo is embroidered in Rose, White and Black as shown on the chart.

To work the duplicate stitch, first thread the yarn onto a blunt-tipped yarn needle. Bring the yarn out, from back to front through the knitting, at the bottom of the stitch to be covered (**1**). Insert the needle at the top of the knitted stitch from right to left under the two 'legs' of the knit stitch above (**2**). Reinsert the needle at the base of the stitch being covered (**3**) to complete the first duplicate stitch. Continue covering stitches along the row in the same way, working across the row from left to right (**4**).

When the embroidery is complete, sew the buttons in place and weave in any stray yarn ends.

TECHNIQUES USED

K1, P1 ribbing –
see page 69
Stocking stitch
Cast-on in middle of a
row – see page 103
Wet blocking – see left
Mattress stitch –
see page 49
Duplicate stitch or
Swiss darning – see left

triangle motif throw

Inspired by modern Scandinavian design, this triangle-motif throw is a stylish investment project, and a great way to hone your colourwork skills. Don't worry about trying to achieve neat sides as the applied i-cord trim tidies up any unsightly edges.

SUPPLIES

SIZE:
Width: 109cm, excluding edging

Length: 132cm, excluding edging

YARN:
Rico *Essentials Big*

Colours: Light Grey (022), Cream (001) and Pistachio (006)

Amount: 14 x 50g balls each of Light Grey and Cream, and 2 balls of Pistachio

KNITTING NEEDLES & EXTRAS:
10mm circular knitting needle, 100cm long

Two 10mm double-pointed knitting needles

TENSION:
11 sts and 14 rows to 10cm (4in) measured over st st colour pattern using 10mm knitting needles.

ABBREVIATIONS:
See either page 14 or the inside back-cover flap.

SPECIAL NOTE:
When working from the colour chart on page 108, read from right to left on the knit (odd-numbered) rows and from left to right on the purl (even-numbered) rows. To switch to another colour, drop the working yarn and change to the second colour. Strand the colour not in use loosely across the wrong side of the work until it is needed again – this creates 'floats' on the wrong side. Avoid pulling the floats too tight as the stitches will pucker at each colour change. When floats need to span more than 5 or 6 stitches, as on rows 1, 4, 5 and 8 of the chart, twist the yarn not in use over the working yarn half way along the section, and continue in the current colour.

TO MAKE THE THROW

Using circular needle and Light Grey, cast on 120 sts.
Begin working back and forth in rows from the colour chart as follows:

Chart row 1 (RS): *K7 in Light Grey, K1 in Cream; rep from * to end.

Chart row 2: P2 in Cream, *P5 in Light Grey, P3 in Cream; rep from * to last 6 sts, ending with P5 in Light Grey, P1 in Cream.

The last two rows set the position of the chart.

Cont in st st working from the chart until all 8 rows of the chart have been completed.

Repeat chart rows 1–8 until your work measures 132cm from cast-on edge, finishing on chart row 4 or 8. Cast off.

TO WORK THE I-CORD EDGING

Using Pistachio, cast on 4 sts onto a double-pointed needle using the single of thumb cast-on method (see page 103, steps 5 and 6). Slide the 4 sts to the right end of the needle and using a second double-pointed needle, work as follows:

Row 1: Pass working yarn behind sts and pulling yarn tight on the first st, K3, sl 1, yo, pick up and knit 1 st from blanket edge (6 sts), pass 4th and 5th sts on right needle together over 6th stitch, as if casting off (4 sts), slide sts to the right end of needle so that working yarn is coming from the left.

Repeat last row all around the throw until you reach first picked up stitch. Cast off.

Cut off yarn, leaving a long yarn tail. Using the yarn tail, sew the ends of the edging together with a basic whip stitch.

Weave in any stray yarn ends.

TO BLOCK THE BLANKET

To set the stitches and smooth the edges of the blanket so it lies flat, block it with a steam iron.

Lay the blanket on a flat surface with a towel underneath. Hold the iron a few centimetres above the knitting and move it slowly over a small section at a time, patting the stitches gently to encourage the process. Pay particular attention to the outside edges.

TECHNIQUES USED

Stranded colourwork
i-cord edging –
see page 92
Whip stitch –
see page 95

KEY

Light Grey – knit on a right side row, purl on a wrong side row

Cream – knit on a right side row, purl on a wrong side row

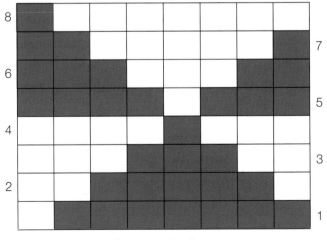

8 st repeat pattern

cotton dishcloth

Hardwearing cotton yarn is perfect for dishcloth duties — pretty neon cotton is even better! It's durable for scrubbing and absorbent enough to mop up spills; just pop the cloth in the washing machine to launder it when things gets messy. These can also be used as pot holders or heat mats

SUPPLIES

SIZE:

Width: 18cm

Length: 18cm

YARN:

Rico *Baby Cotton Soft DK*

Colours: Fuchsia (012) and Beige (004)

Amount: 1 x 50g ball of each colour

KNITTING NEEDLES & EXTRAS:

Pair of 3.5mm knitting needles

15cm of 1.5cm wide cotton ribbon for hanging loop

Sewing needle and cotton sewing thread

TENSION:

30 sts to 10cm (4in) measured over slip-stitch colour pattern using 3.5mm needles.

ABBREVIATIONS:

sl 1 with yarn in front   bring the working yarn to the front of the work between the two needles (as if to purl), slip the next stitch purlwise and return the working yarn to the correct position to continue.

sl 1 with yarn in back   bring the working yarn to the back of the work between the two needles (as if to purl), slip the next stitch purlwise and return the working yarn to the correct position to continue.

See also either page 14 or the inside back-cover flap.

SPECIAL NOTE:

When changing colours between border stitches and pattern stitches, twist the working yarn of each colour around themselves before carrying on in the alternate colour. This will avoid small holes in the finished piece.

When changing colours between rows allow the unused colour to hang at the side of the work and pick it up again when you next need it.

Cut off Beige and cont in Fuchsia.
Work 3 rows in garter st (knit
every row).
Cast off.
Weave in any stray yarn ends.

TO BLOCK THE DISHCLOTH

Pin the dishcloth into a square
shape on an ironing board, or a
clean towel. Hold the iron just over
the surface on a steam setting,
being careful it doesn't touch your
knitting. This will set the stitches and
allow the cloth to lay flat and square.

TO FINISH

Turn under the ends of the
ribbon and fold the ribbon in half
widthways. Using a sewing needle
and sewing thread, sew the hanging
loop to one corner of the dishcloth.

TO MAKE THE DISHCLOTH

Using Fuchsia, cast on 54 sts.
Work 4 rows in garter stitch (knit every row).
Begin slip-stitch colour pattern as follows:
Row 1: K2 in Fuchsia, switch to Beige, *K1, sl 1
with yarn in front; rep from * until 2 sts remain, switch
to Fuchsia (use a separate small ball of Fuchsia for
the 2 border sts on this side of the knitting on
rows 1 and 2), K2.
Row 2: K2 in Fuchsia, switch to Beige, *P1, sl 1 with
yarn in back; rep from * until 2 sts remain, switch to
Fuchsia, K2.
Row 3: Using Fuchsia for entire row, K2, *K1, sl 1 with
yarn in front; rep from * until 2 sts remain, K2.
Row 4: Using Fuchsia for entire row, K2, *P1, sl 1 with
yarn in back; rep from * until 2 sts remain, K2.
Rows 1–4 are repeated to form the pattern.
Cont in pattern until your work measures about 17.5cm
from cast-on edge, ending the last repeat on a row 3.

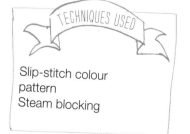

TECHNIQUES USED

Slip-stitch colour
pattern
Steam blocking

chevron cushion

I'm a sucker for geometric patterns and can't resist a good chevron design. This cushion is knitted flat in one piece and then seamed using mattress stitch. It's a good opportunity to practise colourwork and to create a striking home accessory.

SUPPLIES

SIZE:
Width: 40cm

Length: 40cm

YARN:
Debbie Bliss *Cashmerino Aran*

Colours: Lime (502) and Ecru (101)

Amounts: 3 x 50g balls in each colour

KNITTING NEEDLES & EXTRAS:
Pair of 5mm knitting needles

Blunt-tipped yarn needle

Measuring tape

Three 3cm buttons

40cm x 40cm cushion pad

TENSION:
18 sts and 20 rows to 10cm (4in) measured over st st using 5mm needles.

ABBREVIATIONS:
See either page 14 or the inside back-cover flap.

SPECIAL NOTES:
The cover is worked in stocking stitch in colourwork using the stranding technique.

When working from the colour chart on page 117, read from right to left on the knit (odd-numbered) rows and from left to right on the purl (even-numbered) rows.

To switch to another colour, drop the working yarn and change to the second colour. Strand the colour not in use loosely across the wrong side of the work until it is needed again – this creates 'floats' on the wrong side. Avoid pulling the floats too tight as the stitches will pucker at each colour change.

When floats need to span more than 5 or 6 stitches, as on rows 1, 4, 5 and 8 of the chart, twist the yarn not in use over the working yarn half way along the section, and continue in the current colour.

TO MAKE THE CUSHION COVER
Using Lime, cast on 72 sts.

Begin K1, P1 ribbing as follows:

Rib row 1: *K1, P1; rep from * to end.

Repeat last row 8 times more. (A total of 9 rib rows have been worked.)

Begin working from colour chart

Using both Lime and Ecru, begin working in st st from colour chart on page 117 as follows:

Chart row 1 (RS): *K1 in Lime, K7 in Ecru; rep from * to end.

Chart row 2: P1 in Lime, *P5 in Ecru, P3 in Lime; rep from * to last 7 sts, ending with P5 in Ecru, P2 in Lime.

The last two rows set the position of the chart.

Cont in st st working from the chart until all 8 rows of the chart have been completed.

Repeat chart rows 1–8 until your work measures 80cm from the cast-on edge, ending with a chart row 4 or 8. (Approximately 19–20 8-row

repeats of the chart will have been worked.)
Cut off Ecru and continue with Lime.
Knit 1 row.

Next row: *K1, P1; rep from * to end.

Work 3 rows more in K1, P1 ribbing as set, so ending with a WS row.

Buttonholes

Keeping the rib correct as set, work buttonholes over next 2 rows as follows:

Buttonhole row 1: Rib 15 sts, cast off next 4 sts, *work in rib until there are 15 sts on right needle after last cast-off, cast off next 4 sts; rep from * once more, rib to end.

Buttonhole row 2: Keeping rib correct as set, *rib 15 sts, turn work, cast on 4 sts onto the left needle using the knit cast-on, turn work: rep from * twice more, rib to end.
Work 3 rows more in rib. Cast off.

TO BLOCK THE CUSHION COVER

Weave in any stray yarn ends.
As stocking stitch has a tendency to curl at the edges, it is essential that you wet block the knitting to the correct measurements before sewing the side seams. This will also help to smooth out and set the stitches, creating a flawless and professional fabric for your cushion. Submerge the entire piece in tepid water. Let it soak for a few minutes until wet through. Then very carefully lift it from the water supporting the entire weight, so as not to stretch it.

Gently squeeze out excess water without wringing or twisting and place the knitting on a dry towel. Bring together the edges of the towel and press out as much moisture as possible.
Now lay out a clean, dry bath towel on a flat surface. Place the knitting on this towel and pin it to a width of 40cm and a length of 84cm. Leave it to dry.

TO FINISH

Once the work is completely dry, wrap it right side out around the cushion pad with the ribbed edges overlapping. Pin the folded sides loosely to create a square, and mark where you will need to sew, ensuring the stitches line up with the corresponding row. Using mattress stitch, sew each side seam.
Sew the buttons in place.

TECHNIQUES USED

K1, P1 ribbing –
see page 69
Stranded colourwork
Knit cast-on in the middle of a row
Wet blocking –
see page 65
Mattress stitch –
see page 49

KEY

 Lime – knit on a right side row, purl on a wrong side row

 Ecru – knit on a right side row, purl on a wrong side row

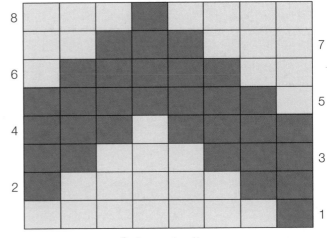

8 st repeat pattern

EGG COSY CAPS

Breakfast in bed just got a little brighter… and cuter! These caps are great for using up those oddments of leftover yarn, and will keep your boiled eggs warm and cosy for longer.

SIZE:
Circumference of cap: 12.5cm

YARN:
Rico *Baby Cotton Soft DK*

Colours: Melon (014), Fuchsia (012), Light Yellow (009) and Mint (015)

Amount: 10g in each colour

KNITTING NEEDLES & EXTRAS:
Set of four 3.75mm double-pointed knitting needles

Stitch marker

2cm pompom maker (or cardboard to make a template)

TENSION:
23 sts and 29 rows to 10cm (4in) measured over st st using 3.75mm needles.

ABBREVIATIONS:
See either page 14 or the inside back-cover flap.

TO MAKE THE CAP
Make one cap in each colour. Cast on 32 sts, using the knit cast-on method. Distribute sts on three needles (10 sts on needle one, 11 sts on needle two, 11 sts on needle three). Place a marker at beg of round and join for working in the round, being careful no sts are twisted. As this is such a small circumference, use needle three to knit the first stitch in the round 1, then change to needle four to continue.

Rounds 1, 2, 3, 4 and 5: *K1, P1; rep from * to end.
Rounds 6, 7, 8 and 9: Knit.
Round 10: [K6, K2tog] 4 times. (28 sts)
Round 11: Knit.
Round 12: [K5, K2tog] 4 times. (24 sts)
Round 13: Knit.
Round 14: [K4, K2tog] 4 times. (20 sts)
Round 15: Knit.
Round 16: [K3, K2tog] 4 times. (16 sts)

Round 17: Knit.
Round 18: [K2, K2tog] 4 times.
(12 sts)
Cut off yarn, leaving a long yarn
tail. Thread the yarn tail onto a yarn
needle, pass the needle through the
remaining live stitches, pull to draw
closed and secure. Leave the yarn
tail to use to sew the mini pompom
to the top of the cap.

TO MAKE THE POMPOM

Make one 4cm pompom in each
colour. If you do not have a
pompom maker, cut two identical
cardboard rings, each 6cm in
diameter and with a hole in the
centre 2cm in diameter. Place the
two rings together.

Now using the pompom maker or
the cardboard rings, thread the yarn
round and round the rings (**1**) – the
more yarn you use, the thicker
the pompom will be. Holding the
wrapped rings securely, cut the
yarn around the edge of the rings,
inserting the scissor tip between the
rings as you cut (**2** and **3**).

Tie a long length of yarn securely
around the centre of the strands
between the rings (**4**), pull tightly
and knot. Gently remove the
pompom from the rings and fluff
up the pompom. Trim into shape if
necessary (**5**).

Using the long yarn tail on the cap,
sew the pompom to the centre of
the top of the cap.

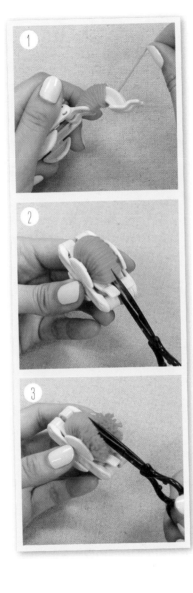

TECHNIQUES USED

Knit cast-on – see page 20
Working in the round –
see page 44
K2tog – see pages 28–29
Making pompoms –
see left

hedgehog paperweight

Meet Harry. He's a hedgehog. And he's ready to serve all your desk-related needs… just as long as they involve sitting on your important papers all day. He loves doing this very much – almost as much as he loves the occasional biscuit!

SUPPLIES

SIZE:
Width: 8cm

Length: 13cm

YARN:
Rico *Essentials Merino DK*

Colours: Rust (51), Natural (60) and Black (90)

Amounts: 1 x 50g ball each of Rust and Natural, and small amount in Black

KNITTING NEEDLES & EXTRAS:
Set of four 3.75mm double-pointed knitting needles

Polyester fiberfill (toy stuffing)

100g of small, weighted poly pellets (for toy making)

Small plastic bag to contain pellets

Stitch marker

TECHNIQUES USED

Working in the round – see page 44

Loopy stitch – see page 124

KFB – see pages 32–33

K2tog – see pages 28–29

SSK – see page 52

TENSION:
24 sts and 32 rows to 10cm (4in) measured over st st using 3.75mm needles.

ABBREVIATIONS:
loopy stitch   See page 124.

See also either page 14 or the inside back-cover flap.

TO MAKE THE PAPERWEIGHT
Using Rust, cast on 6 sts. Distribute sts evenly on three double-pointed needles (2 sts on each needle). Place a marker at beg of round and join for working in the round, being careful no stitches are twisted.

Body

Round 1: [KFB] 6 times. (12 sts)

Round 2: Work in loopy stitch.

Round 3: [KFB, K1] 6 times. (18 sts)

Round 4: Work in loopy stitch.

Round 5: [KFB, K2] 6 times. (24 sts)

Round 6: Work in loopy stitch.

Round 7: [KFB, K3] 6 times. (30 sts)

Round 8: Work in loopy stitch.

Round 9: Knit.

[Repeat rounds 8 and 9] 6 times more, then repeat round 8 once more. (11 loopy stitch rounds have been worked in total)

Now add toy stuffing to fill out the body. Place the weighted pellets in a small plastic bag and tie the bag closed. Insert the pellet bag inside the toy stuffing.

Shape face

Cut off Rust and continue in Natural, adding more toy stuffing as you proceed.

Round 1: K30.

Round 2: K2tog, K16, SSK, K10. (28 sts)

Round 3 and all odd rounds: Knit.

Round 4: K2tog, K14, SSK, K4, K2tog, K4. (25 sts)

Round 6: K2tog, K12, SSK, K4, K2tog, K3. (22 sts)

Round 8: K2tog, K10, SSK, K3, K2tog, K3. (19 sts)

Round 10: K2tog, K8, SSK, K3, K2tog, K2. (16 sts)

Round 12: K2tog, K6, SSK, K2, K2tog, K2. (13 sts)

Round 14: K2tog, K4, SSK, K2, K2tog, K1. (10 sts)

Round 16: K2tog, K2, SSK, K1, K2tog, K1. (7 sts)

Round 18: [K2tog] twice, K1, K2tog. (4 sts)
Cut off yarn, leaving a long tail. Thread yarn tail onto a yarn needle, pass the needle through the remaining live stitches, pull to draw closed and secure.

TO MAKE THE EARS

There are three lines of decreases on the top of the head. Mark the ear positions on the top of the head along the top of the last loop row, 3cm apart. Using Rust and with top of head facing you, pick up and knit 3 sts at one ear position.

Row 1: P3.
Row 2: K3.
Row 3: P3.
Row 4: K3tog and fasten off.
Work another ear in the same way.

TO FINISH

Using Black, embroider two little eyes and a nose as shown.
Weave in any stray yarn ends.

WORKING THE LOOPY STITCH

Knit the next stitch, but don't slip it off the left needle (**1** and **2**); bring the working yarn to the front of the work between the two needles, then place the left thumb on top of the working yarn and loop the yarn around the thumb and to the back between the two needles (**3**); keeping the thumb in the loop, insert the left needle through the front loop of the stitch on the right needle and insert the right needle through the back loop of the stitch on the left needle, and knit these 2 stitches together (**4** and **5**). Repeat in each stitch to the end of the round. Work a loopy stitch round and a knit round alternately to form the pattern.

choosing yarns

The yarns recommended for the knitting projects in this book are listed here, with their specifications. It is always best to use the yarn recommended in the knitting pattern in order to achieve the result shown. If you decide to use a substitute yarn for any of the items in this book, find one that is similar in weight, texture and fibre content. To determine the weight (thickness) of a yarn, take into account the generic description of the weight and the manufacturer's recommended tension. Be sure to calculate the amount of substitute yarn you will need by metres (yards) per ball, not by grams.

Debbie Bliss Cashmerino Aran
An Aran-weight yarn; 55% extra-fine merino wool, 35% microfibre, 12% cashmere; 90m (98yd) per 50g (1^3/$_4$oz) ball; recommended tension – 18 sts and 24 rows to 10cm (4in) over st st using 5mm (US size 8) needles.

Debbie Bliss Luxury Donegal Tweed Chunky
A chunky-weight yarn; 90% merino wool, 10% angora; 100m (109yd) per 100g (3^1/$_2$oz) ball; recommended tension – 12 sts and 19 rows to 10cm (4in) over st using 6.5mm (US size 10^1/$_2$) needles.

Debbie Bliss Rialto Chunky
A chunky-weight yarn; 100% merino wool; 60m (66yd) per 50g (1^3/$_4$oz) ball; recommended tension – 15 sts and 21 rows to 10cm (4in) over st st using 6.5mm (US size 10^1/$_2$) needles.

Erika Knight Blue Wool
A double-knitting-weight wool yarn; 100% wool; 55m (60yd) per 25g (^{7}/$_8$oz) ball; recommended tension – 22 sts and 30 rows to 10cm (4in) over st st using 4mm (US size 6) needles.

Erika Knight Maxi Wool
A super-chunky yarn; 100% wool; 80m (87yd) per 100g (3^1/$_2$oz) ball; recommended tension – 8 sts and 12 rows to 10cm (4in) over st st using 12mm (US size 17) needles.

Erika Knight Vintage Wool
An Aran-weight wool yarn; 100% wool; 87m (95yd) per 50g (1^3/$_4$oz) ball; recommended tension – 18 sts and 24 rows to 10cm (4in) over st st using 5mm (US size 8) needles.

King Cole Bamboo Cotton DK
A double-knitting-weight yarn; 50% bamboo, 50% cotton; 230m (251yd) per 100g (3^1/$_2$oz) ball; recommended tension – 22 sts and 30 rows to 10cm (4in) over st st using 4mm (US size 6) needles.

Rico Creative Twist Super Chunky
A super-chunky-weight yarn; 80% acrylic, 20% alpaca; 75m (82yd) per 100g (3^1/$_2$oz) ball; recommended tension – 9 sts and 12 rows to 10cm (4in) over st st using 10mm (US size 15) needles.

Rico Essentials Big
A chunky-weight yarn; 50% wool, 50% acrylic; 48m (52yd) per 50g (1^3/$_4$oz) ball; recommended tension – 11 sts and 16 rows to 10cm (4in) over st st using 7–8mm (US size 10^1/$_2$–11) needles.

Rico Essentials Cotton Soft DK
A double-knitting-weight yarn; 50% cotton, 50% acrylic; 125m (136yd) per 50g (1^3/$_4$oz) ball; recommended tension – 22 sts and 28 rows to 10cm (4in) over st st using 4mm (US size 6) needles.

Rico Essentials Merino DK
A double-knitting-weight yarn; 100% wool; 120m (131yd) per 50g (1^3/$_4$oz) ball; recommended tension – 22 sts and 28 rows to 10cm (4in) over st st using 4mm (US size 6) needles.

Rico Essentials Soft Merino Aran
An Aran-weight yarn; 100% merino wool; 100m (109yd) per 50g (1^3/$_4$oz) ball; recommended tension – 18 sts and 24 rows to 10cm (4in) over st st using 5mm (US size 8) needles.

Rowan Wool Cotton DK
A double-knitting-weight yarn; 50% cotton, 50% merino wool; 113m (123yd) per 50g (1^3/$_4$oz) ball; recommended tension – 22–24 sts and 30–32 rows to 10cm (4in) over st st using 3.75–4mm (US size 5–6) needles.

Sirdar Flirt DK
A double-knitting-weight wool yarn; 80% bamboo sourced viscose, 20% wool; 95m (104yd) per 50g (1^3/$_4$oz) ball; recommended tension – 22 sts and 28 rows to 10cm (4in) over st st using 4mm (US size 6) needles.

Sirdar Snuggly Baby Bamboo DK
Same description and specifications as Sirdar *Flirt DK.*

index

THANK YOU THANK YOU THANK YOU

A very big thank you to Lisa at Quadrille for giving me the opportunity to write this book; and to Christine, Keiko, Gemma and Chinh for all their hard work making it happen — a wonderful team to work with!

To Ben for buying me my very first knitting book, and for always being there to listen to my ideas, offer constructive opinions, and keep me motivated along the way.

To my family — Mum, Dad and Alsie for their unwavering support and encouragement.

Thank you also to Debbie Bliss, Erika Knight and Rico for providing yarn for the majority of the projects.

Publishing Director Jane O'Shea
Commissioning Editor Lisa Pendreigh
Editor Sally Harding
Creative Director Helen Lewis
Art Direction & Design Claire Peters
Designer Gemma Hogan
Photographer Keiko Oikawa
Stylist and Illustrator Christine Leech
Production Director Vincent Smith
Production Controller Aysun Hughes

Quadrille
craft

www.quadrillecraft.com

First published in 2014 by
Quadrille Publishing Ltd
Alhambra House
27–31 Charing Cross Road
London WC2H 0LS
www.quadrille.co.uk

Text and project designs © 2014 Jessica Biscoe
Photography © 2014 Keiko Oikawa
Illustrations © 2014 Christine Leech
Design & layout © 2014 Quadrille Publishing Ltd

British Library Cataloguing-in-Publication Data. A catalogue record for this book is available from the British Library.

ISBN: 978 184949 463 2

Printed in China.